TRUE ST

D0541439

WORLD WAR II

Clive Gifford

Illustrations by John Yates

Published in 2013 by Wayland
Text copyright © Clive Gifford 2013
Illustrations © Wayland 2013

Wayland
338 Euston Road
London NW1 3BH

Wayland Australia
Level 17/207 Kent Street
Sydney, NSW 2000

Cover design: Lisa Peacock
Cover illustration: Maddox Philpott
Book design by Don Martin
Edited by Kelly Davis

A CIP catalogue record for this book is available
from the British Library.

ISBN 978 0 7502 8045 7

2 4 6 8 10 9 7 5 3 1

Printed and bound by CPI Group (UK) Ltd, Croydon, CRO 4YY

First published in 2002 by Hodder Children's Books

Wayland is a division of Hachette Children's Books,
an Hachette UK Company
www.hachette.co.uk

Contents

Author's Note

Truth really can be stranger than fiction, and more exciting, astonishing and compelling as well. I hope you will agree that these nine true stories from World War II prove the point.

They feature soldiers, sailors, airmen and civilians from both sides but what links them is that they all record acts of incredible daring, resolve, bravery and compassion. The stories have been compiled from lots of different sources, including previously published accounts, letters and diaries. I spent many fascinating days in museum and library archives, talking to historians and receiving kind assistance from experts and relatives.

I hope you find reading the stories as interesting and inspiring as I found researching and writing them.

Clive

Clive Gifford

CHAPTER 1

Through the Eye of a Needle

Germany knew better than most nations the power and potential of submarines in battle. In World War I, their early, primitively designed U-boats had sunk over 800 vessels. Britain, Germany's enemy, was an island, dependent on goods and supplies sent across the sea. So, in World War II, it made sense to attack Britain's shipping, both military and merchant.

The newly formed German submarine force, the Kreigsmarine, was commanded by a master tactician. He hand-picked one of his most able captains to perform an incredibly daring mission right in the heart of enemy waters.

❖　❖　❖

Günther Prien left the office of his commander, Karl Dönitz, with his mind in a whirl. What the former World War I U-boat captain, now head of Germany's new submarine force, had told him was mindblowing. Dönitz was convinced that Scapa Flow, the heavily guarded harbour used by the British Royal Navy, had weaknesses. According to him, a single German submarine could penetrate the harbour's defences. That submarine was to be Prien's own vessel, *U-47*.

Scapa Flow lay in the Orkney Islands, north of the northernmost tip of Scotland. It had been a major British harbour for over 100 years and many of the Royal Navy's most famous battleships and cruisers had moored there. Several German submarines had travelled close to Scapa Flow to map the harbour in secret. Dönitz believed that a lone U-boat could get through the defences and attack the British fleet at rest when they would be least expecting it.

Such a surprise raid would not only enable the Germans to sink one or two enemy ships. More importantly, it would also damage British morale. World War II had started little more than a month earlier and Dönitz had just a fifth of the subs he felt were necessary to form a strong fighting unit. If this mission was successful, he was convinced that Hitler would be impressed enough to speed up

U-boat building and crew training.

Günther Prien had joined the German Navy just as the country, under the Nazis, started to re-arm in the 1930s. In 1935, he volunteered for the newly formed submarine force and eventually gained command of his own craft, the very latest German submarine, a Type VIIB U-boat.

Born to a poor family in Leipzig, he had struggled through much hardship as a child and teenager. His childhood hero had been the Portuguese sailor and explorer, Vasco da Gama; and, at the age of sixteen, Prien had left home for a life on the sea. He had started his naval career as a cabin boy, gradually working his way up to captain his own merchant ship, ferrying goods and supplies around the seas. Prien never forgot his humble beginnings and was popular with his crew who respected his skill and strong nerve when in danger. He would need all his courage on the mission ahead.

On 8 October, Prien and his 43-strong crew headed out of the harbour at Kiel, travelled along the Kiel Canal and entered the southernmost part of the North Sea. By day, the submarine ran underwater. By night, it travelled along the surface. On 12 October, *U-47* reached the Orkneys.

Prien's crew had suspected a special mission right from the start but only now, moored just 40 metres away from British land, did they receive the full details. All crew members were forbidden to smoke, and they were only to talk when absolutely necessary and then in whispers. Scuttling charges were placed all over the submarine. These special explosives would be detonated to sink *U-47* should it find itself cornered with no hope of escape. Some of the crew were fearful, many were surprised, but all set to their tasks with grim determination. They were going to strike at the very centre of the enemy's navy and they were completely, utterly alone.

U-47 approached the entrance to the harbour. Prien ordered the submarine to surface so that they could choose their final passage through the heavily fortified waters of the harbour. The looming shapes of two ships, the *Thames* and the *Soriano*, dominated the view ahead. These block ships had been placed there to act as a barricade, and it would be difficult and dangerous to pass between them. If Prien doubted whether his submarine could continue without being spotted, he didn't let on to any of his crew.

Prien took control and attempted to guide the U-boat through the narrow channel between the two ships, the tides and sea currents making the task especially hazardous. Suddenly the anchor chain of one of the ships appeared in view. Prien adjusted his sub's rudder to steer him clear of the chain but the currents were against him. The crew heard the terrifying sound of their vessel grating on the steel anchor chain. In seconds, the *U-47* would be forced into the side of one of the block ships.

Prien struggled with the rudder and then emptied the air tanks to force the submarine down and away from the ships. The sub's hull scraped against the rocks on the side and bottom of the channel, but just after midnight, the *U-47* was through. Prien wrote in his diary, 'Wir sind in Scapa Flow!!!' – 'We are in Scapa Flow!!!'. His excitement was understandable; he had managed to thread his craft 'through the eye of a needle' and into the harbour. Yet there was still much to do. Prien ordered the *U-47* to cruise slowly and steathily through the harbour waters, scouting for prey.

Excitement and relief quickly turned to fear and desperation as no targets could be found. Where German sources had reported a harbour full of craft, Prien discovered nothing more than inky blackness. The natural harbour of Scapa Flow was huge. Prien and his crew had to wait many tense minutes as the submarine travelled through the enemy waters in search of prey. Some of the crew were beginning to lose their nerve. But not Prien. Dönitz had chosen his mission commander very well. Prien had a steely resolve and an ability to sum up situations very rapidly.

It was about 1 a.m. when Prien spotted the battleship, *Royal Oak*, in his periscope viewfinder. Downing the scope, he ordered the torpedo tubes to be primed and a salvo of three torpedoes aimed and fired, two at the *Royal Oak* and a third at a vessel Prien had located just beyond the battleship. The submarine gave a small shudder as it discharged its lethal weapons into the cold sea. With the British battleship some 3,000 metres away, the *U-47*'s torpedoes were close to their maximum range. They had the 'legs' to reach their target but would they hit it?

The delay was almost unbearable. Imagine firing a weapon and having to wait three and a half minutes before you knew whether you had hit or missed your target. Now, place yourself deep in enemy territory, metres underwater, without the speed or armaments to escape easily.

That was the situation facing Prien and the forty-three other crew members of *U-47*. They waited and waited. Seconds seemed like minutes, minutes like whole hours. Suddenly, a giant fountain of water erupted from the calm surface of the harbour. The *Royal Oak* had been hit but Prien wasn't convinced they had dealt it a fatal blow. Another salvo of three torpedoes was fired. This time, there was no doubt. The explosions lifted the enormous battleship partly out of the water. Flames blazed high into the night sky. Within minutes, the *Royal Oak* started to slide slowly beneath the water. Prien gave the orders for *U-47* to turn away and try to escape. The excitement the crew had felt as the *Royal Oak* had been hit, now dissolved into a crackling tension. With the British forces on full alert, could they really find a way through the natural and manned defences of the harbour and sail free?

Prien decided to navigate his submarine through a second, trickier route out of the harbour. The southern channel was even narrower than the way in but there were no block ships in the way. Prien's knuckles were white and his forehead glistened with sweat as he carefully guided his craft along the hazardous route out of Scapa Flow. Several times, the submarine scraped against the rocky sides and edges of the channel and nearly ran aground. But by 2.15 a.m., *U-47* was free, out in the deep waters of the North Sea.

A crate of beer was opened and the crew celebrated. A single 740 tonne submarine had managed to sneak into and out of the British Royal Navy's main harbour, sinking a 30,000 tonne battleship for the loss of no German life. The crew nicknamed their craft 'the bull of Scapa Flow' and daubed the outline of a snorting bull in red paint on the submarine's conning tower (the tallest part of the vessel, used for steering and firing when near the surface).

U-47's trip back to its German base at Wilhelmshaven took three days, and the journey wasn't exactly peaceful. On one occasion, British minesweeper ships spotted the submarine in the distance and gave chase. Commander Prien had to crash-dive his U-boat, forcing it down sharply into the ocean depths. The minesweepers fired depth charges into the water nearby but, fortunately for *U-47*, it escaped without harm.

Prien and his crew arrived back in Germany to a heroes' welcome. They met and had dinner with Adolf Hitler who awarded each member of the entire crew the Iron Cross (Second Class) and Prien the Knight's Cross of the Iron Cross.

❖ ❖ ❖

Just seven weeks into World War II, the German Kriegsmarine had scored a significant victory. The *Royal Oak* was not the finest ship in Britain's Royal Navy. It had been built in 1916 and was slow and unwieldy. But its loss – along with over 800 of its crew – was a tragedy and shook Britain's leaders.

Yet the real damage done to the Royal Navy only became clear later on. The British forces had been surprised by the attack; they realized they needed to construct tighter defences around Scapa Flow. Shipping had to be moved to other harbours, and Dönitz then instructed German submarines to lay mines in these other, less-guarded places. These mines caused severe damage to the cruiser, HMS *Belfast*, and the battleship, HMS *Nelson*.

After their successful raid at Scapa Flow, the crew of *U-47* continued to attack convoys of supply ships in the North Atlantic until spring 1941. *U-47* managed to sink a further twenty-four ships and Prien was again called to meet Hitler and be decorated with medals. Dönitz, Prien's commander, offered the *U-47*'s captain a place away from the dangers of combat. He could start straight away, training other U-boat commanders but Prien insisted on remaining in charge of his beloved submarine.

On 6 March 1941, Prien attacked another shipping convoy in the Atlantic ocean. It was the last success for the 'bull of Scapa Flow'. Two days later, *U-47* was sunk, with the loss of Prien and all his crew. For many years, the British destroyer *Wolverine* was credited with the sinking of *U-47* but, more recently, some evidence has emerged that the famous submarine may have been sunk by one of its own faulty, circling torpedoes.

Whatever the cause of its sinking, *U-47* and Günther Prien will remain best known for sneaking through the formidable defences of the Royal Navy's premier harbour – when Germany's 'bull' got in to Britain's backyard.

◆ ◆ ◆

CHAPTER 2

The Ultimate Sacrifice

As the Germans swept through France in the early stages of the war, some French soldiers were able to flee to Britain where they joined the Free French forces who fought in many places, including North Africa. Many of the people of the occupied lands stayed in their homes but organized underground groups who worked in secret to help the Allies and undermine the German forces. Known as the resistance, they played a vital part in the war, reporting German troop and vehicle movements to the Allies, destroying vital enemy installations, and helping Allied prisoners of war escape back to their own countries. The Special Operations Executive (SOE) was a small, highly trained Allied force which aided, assisted and co-ordinated the resistance and underground groups so that their efforts had even more impact. One of the few women in this elite band to go into enemy territory was Violette Szabo.

◆　◆　◆

It was a long, slow, four-hour flight from Cambridge to northern France in the rumbling American Liberator aircraft. The four SOE personnel, known as special operatives, sat on the floor of the bomber plane drinking coffee from flasks and playing gin rummy. The pilot and his crew were amazed at their calm. These four would shortly parachute deep into German-held territory and make contact with the local maquis – the term for a French resistance group. There, right under the noses of German soldiers, they were to perform top secret missions to disrupt the German forces.

Among the four were Captain Charles Staunton, whose real name was Philippe Liewer, and a 22-year-old woman, born to a French mother and an English father, codenamed 'Louise'. Small and slender but with a fiery passion blazing in her eyes, this woman was one of a handful of female operatives sent into occupied territories to help the resistance. Her name was Violette Szabo.

She had been born Violette Bushell but had met and married a member of the Free French forces, Etienne Szabo, four years earlier. The couple had a daughter called Tanya, and were very happy together. But Etienne had been killed at the Battle of El Alamein in North Africa, and, after a period of grief, Violette had become determined to do all that she could to avenge her husband's death and help the Allied war effort.

While working at an anti-aircraft gun battery, her intelligence and quick thinking had been noticed by the authorities. Some time after Etienne's death, Violette was called up to London for a series of mysterious interviews and tests. Slowly, gradually, what she was being tested for became clear. The work she would do as a member of the Special Operations Executive would be top secret and very dangerous. She was given every opportunity to refuse but immediately leapt at the chance.

This June 1944 mission was Violette's second into enemy territory. Her first had been a nerve-racking journey to Normandy, Rouen, and – finally – Paris. She had been sent in to Rouen to help rebuild a resistance group and had only narrowly evaded capture. But this second mission was even more important. It was 7 June 1944 and the D-Day landings on the beaches of Normandy were catching the Germans by surprise. Large numbers of German troops and tanks would soon be heading north towards Normandy. The resistance would do their best to disrupt their journey.

Shortly before they parachuted down, the four sang a popular song of the day, 'I'll Be Around'. The crew of the plane thought they had gone mad but it was a theme song for many of those who went in behind enemy lines. They just hoped they would meet again to sing it with each other back in England.

❖ ❖ ❖

The four parachuted down safely and made contact with the local resistance group based in the village of Sussac, near the town of Limoges, some distance south of Normandy. One of the leaders, whose real name was Jacques Dufor, had the codename 'Anastasie'. The Germans were after Anastasie. They viewed him as 'the most dangerous bandit' in the area. He had been involved in many resistance raids, and possessed vital knowledge of the area and other resistance groups. A formidable Panzer division of the best German tanks would soon be travelling through the area towards Normandy. Staunton, Anastasie and others made plans to attack the routes along which this tank division would travel.

Anastasie insisted on going with Violette to deliver the plan to other, nearby resistance groups who might be suspicious without his word and attendance. The Frenchman was a key part of the plan and Violette knew he had to be protected at all costs.

On 10 June, Violette and Anastasie, with their weapons close at hand, drove out of Sussac. Their journey through the picturesque French countryside started peacefully enough. They had chosen the safest route they could find; it took them through the village of Salon-le-Tour, where Anastasie had lived as a child. As they entered the village, Anastasie pointed out some of its sights before bringing the car sharply to a halt. He had spotted some Germans.

Anastasie was too well-known for the pair to pretend that they were innocent travellers. Grabbing their weapons, they quickly stole out of the car. Some of the Germans spotted them and opened fire. Anastasie threw himself into the ditch by the roadside. Violette stood tall and shot back with her Sten machine gun.

Anastasie shouted at her to follow him into the ditch. More and more German soldiers started to appear in the distance. Unleashing another volley of bullets, Violette quickly followed Anastasie. The pair scuttled along the shallow ditch and past some farm outbuildings, both occasionally stopping to return fire.

The Germans were from an advanced detachment of the Das Reich division. Their job was to scour the countryside ahead of the main force of tanks and troops, making sure that the path was clear. They numbered over 400 and were well-trained and well-armed.

Violette and Anastasie ran for their lives, waded through a stream and raced through a cornfield. Behind them, the German soldiers in two armoured cars and on foot were speeding after them. The air was hot with machine-gun fire. A bullet tore through Anastasie's jacket but missed his body. Violette received a flesh wound from a bullet which grazed her as it went flying past. The pair of them darted this way and that through the cornfield. The quickest way forward was a straight line, but that would be suicide, as it would leave a straight path for their pursuers, armed with machine guns and rifles.

Suddenly Violette fell to the ground. A sharp bolt of pain exploded all the way up her leg. Her ankle, weakened by several hard parachute falls in training, was badly twisted. There was no way she could go on. Anastasie whirled round. Violette insisted he carry on without her, but he would not hear of it. Instead, he picked her up and continued to run.

Violette begged him to leave her. She beat his chest and shoulders with her fists as Anastasie stumbled on much more slowly than before, carrying her in his arms. With one huge lurch, Violette forced them both to the ground and rolled away from Anastasie. 'Run!' she shouted. Anastasie was vital to the entire mission. He might still escape without her. Anastasie paused, but Violette insisted he go on by himself. She quickly moved away from him, half-scrambling, half-limping out of the cornfield and to the shelter of a nearby tree. She had already fitted a new magazine of bullets to her Sten gun and was firing. Anastasie took one last look at his brave colleague before sprinting away.

❖　❖　❖

Violette unclicked another spent container of bullets, threw it away and fitted a fresh one. Her chances of escape were zero. Bullets ripped the air around her. Some struck nearby trees and even the one she was partly sheltering behind. All she could now think of was attracting attention to herself and away from Anastasie. By firing at the advancing soldiers she also hoped to slow them down enough for Anastasie to escape or hide.

As the German soldiers closed in on Violette, she emptied round after round of bullets at the advancing enemy. To this day, no one knows how many she killed or wounded but witnesses saw many Germans fall. Violette was considered the best shot in the whole of the SOE, and, when times had been hard for her in London, she had won cigarettes and prizes by visiting shooting galleries where she always won.

She reached for another magazine full of bullets, but there were none left. The Germans were almost upon her now. There was nothing she could do to stop them. She fought them with her fists, her feet and teeth, but she was exhausted and in pain. The soldiers quickly overpowered her and held her. The officer of one of the armoured cars strode up and congratulated her on her spirit. Violette was filled with hatred for what the Germans were doing to her mother's home country and for their killing of her husband. She spat at the officer, before she was led away.

The remaining German forces gathered up their wounded, and made a thorough search of the area. They were trying to find Anastasie but Violette's actions had bought the resistance leader enough time to hide. He had continued his zig-zagging run through the cornfield to a small farmhouse, where he had dived under a pile of logs and prayed he would not be found.

As luck would have it, inside the farmhouse were several people who recognized him. When the German soldiers came, a girl who had gone to school with Anastasie sat on the logs to cover any view of the hidden resistance leader. She had been asked if she had seen Anastasie and had shaken her head all the time, keeping her body between the German soldiers and part of the Frenchman's foot which was sticking out from the log pile.

Anastasie eventually made it back to safety and the resistance's plans were carried out successfully. Roads and railway lines were torn up, covered in piles of rocks, or damaged by explosives so badly that they took weeks to repair. The tank division never reached Normandy and other reinforcements sent to fight the D-Day landings were hampered in their journeys as well.

❖   ❖   ❖

In her cell, first in the French town of Limoges, and then in Fresnes, near Paris, Violette couldn't be certain but hoped that their plans had been successful. She thought much of her dead husband, Etienne, of their daughter, Tanya, and of her parents and friends back in England. She feared she would never see them again but she knew her war effort was not yet over. In many ways, she knew that her hardest mission was still to come.

Each day she was dragged from her cell in Limoges and questioned for long periods by the Colonel of the German secret police there. Despite tricks and threats, she told him nothing. Staunton and the other resistance leaders in the area hatched a plan to rescue Szabo from the prison but their hopes were dashed when, the morning before they were to try and seize her, Violette was moved to a much larger prison in Fresnes, near Paris. Then she was taken to one of the most notorious headquarters of the Gestapo (the German secret police), No. 84 Avenue Foch in the centre of Paris.

Here, the questioning became more intense and the conditions worse. The Gestapo showed Szabo no mercy. Underground or resistance workers were treated in a similar way to spies. Whereas captured uniformed soldiers, sailors and air crews were usually reasonably treated, spies were interrogated and tortured until they were broken and gave away vital secrets.

At the beginning, the Gestapo chief was friendly. He offered her a deal. If she gave him the names he wanted, her life would be saved as well as all of those she named. But Violette refused. She never hid the fact that she knew the answers to many of the questions her interrogators asked her. She also made it clear that she had no intention of ever answering them.

As a result, she had to endure the most excruciating torture. But endure it she did, without giving her inquisitors any information which would endanger the lives of her colleagues or prevent their plans from working. With the Allied forces advancing from Normandy into the rest of France, the Gestapo gave up on Violette. She, along with many other prisoners, was moved east into Germany.

❖   ❖   ❖

As Violette stepped off the vehicle which had carried her deep into Germany, she was hit and whipped by female German camp guards. Then she was bundled inside, stripped, and forced to take a freezing cold shower. She was at the infamous Ravensbruck prison camp, the largest ever prison camp for women.

When Ravensbruck was built on rotting marshland, 80 kilometres from Berlin, it was designed to hold a maximum of 7,000 female prisoners. By the time Violette arrived, at the end of August 1944, it held 40,000 women, often crammed six to a bed. Those held were Jews, Poles and other victims of the Nazis. The conditions were absolutely appalling. There were few toilets, little clean water, and rats ran freely through the camp. With food shortages throughout Germany, the prisoners only received scraps of food. There was next to no medical help and, as a result of the dreadful conditions, around sixty prisoners died each day.

❖　❖　❖

Violette twice attempted to escape and was twice captured and punished. Locked away in a cramped cubicle in a concrete bunker, as punishment, she received one hot meal every three days and no other food. Compared to others, her health remained good and, for a time, she was sent to Königsburg on the Russian front. There, she and two other captured English agents, Lilian Rolfe and Denise Bloch, were forced to fell trees and clear land for a new airfield. They were expected to work as hard as men, and were beaten if they slackened.

Even in such horrific conditions, Violette did her best to raise the spirits of her fellow prisoners and help them when she could. Whatever inner torment she felt, she never showed the German guards any sign of weakness. At the end of January 1945, Szabo, Rolfe and Bloch were ferried back to Ravensbruck. There, the three brave women were shot and their remains cremated, just weeks before the Ravensbruck camp was liberated by Russian forces.

❖ ❖ ❖

Violette Szabo was awarded the George Cross after her death, in 1946. Her parents and daughter, Tanya, received her medal from the King of England, George VI. The bravery of Violette Szabo became more widely known when her story was made into a film, called *Carve Her Name With Pride*. Fifty-five years after her death, a museum in her honour was opened, created by Miss Rosemary E. Rigby MBE at the house where Violette had spent many happy days as a young girl, in Cartref, near Wormelow in Herefordshire.

◆ ◆ ◆

CHAPTER 3

Operation Valkyrie

By 1942, a number of senior German officers had doubts about their leader, Adolf Hitler. The war against the Allied powers was not going well and Hitler's decision to invade Russia was proving disastrous. News of the systematic killing of thousands of Jews was filtering through to senior soldiers, some of whom were horrified. However, most of them either felt powerless to do anything, or remained bound by their oath of loyalty to Hitler and Germany.

A group of brave senior officers felt otherwise. One of their leaders, a much-decorated war hero, was prepared to lead from the front. A favourite of Hitler's, he was personally prepared to carry, arm and place the bomb designed to kill his country's leader. That man was Count Claus Schenk von Stauffenberg.

◆ ◆ ◆

The German officer lay in a hospital in Munich, his body in tatters. He had lost his right hand, two fingers from his left, and the use of his left eye. In addition, his hearing was damaged and his legs were twisted and mangled. The doctors were convinced that, if he survived, he would never walk again.

But the doctors had not reckoned with the incredible spirit of Claus von Stauffenberg. The German officer clawed his way back to life and forced himself – with blazing determination – to re-learn basic skills. Despite having only three fingers and an arm stump to work with, he was soon capable of washing, dressing and feeding himself. He even worked on developing special versions of tools, such as pliers, which he could operate with the three fingers remaining on his left hand. By the summer of 1943, he amazed doctors by walking again, and within weeks he asked to be sent to the front.

Most people assumed that Stauffenberg was driven by his desire to serve Hitler and the Nazi cause. But nothing could have been further from the truth. Stauffenberg now wished to be an important part of the movement that would depose Hitler and possibly bring the war to an end.

❖   ❖   ❖

Born to an aristocratic family, Stauffenberg was already a soldier when Hitler came to power in 1933. Although the young count felt the war had been unnecessary from the start, he still served loyally and with great success. He rose through the ranks but he became more and more disgusted with the poor leadership of the German forces and with the extreme racism of its leader who seemed determined to kill the entire Jewish race.

The German resistance movement had been working underground for some time when the war hero with the eye patch and missing hand arrived to join their ranks. Stauffenberg was tired of talk, he wanted action, and he was prepared to take the lead in any attempt to overthrow the Nazis.

By 1944, the conspirators had decided upon a course of action. It involved taking a top secret Nazi plan, called Operation Valkyrie, and using it against those it was designed to protect. Operation Valkyrie gave the German Home Army – the soldiers and officers within Germany – orders to take over all airfields, government buildings and other important facilities if a rebellion occurred within Germany.

Many important people in the Home Army, including its second-in-command, General Friedrich Olbricht, knew about the plot to overthrow Hitler. When Operation Valkyrie was launched, the conspirators planned to use it to arrest Nazis loyal to Hitler and quickly take control of much of Germany. (They had tried to convince the Home Army's leader, General Friedrich Fromm, to join them. Although he refused, he did not tell Hitler of the plotting.)

For the conspirators' plans to work, Hitler had to be eliminated. Too many soldiers would blindly follow the Führer if he was still alive. But there had been other failed assassination attempts, and Hitler was now holed up in his heavily guarded base at Rastenberg, over 600 kilometres away from Berlin.

❖ ❖ ❖

On 1 July 1944, Stauffenberg was promoted to the rank of colonel and took up his new duties as Chief of Staff of the German Home Army. He was now effectively third in command, just below Fromm and Olbricht. More importantly, he would soon be in a position to get access to Hitler.

After several false starts, Stauffenberg received orders to visit Hitler's headquarters to attend a high-level military briefing on 20 July 1944. The conspirators readied themselves. Now was their moment. Stauffenberg would plant the bombs that would kill Hitler and immediately fly back to Berlin where he would be an important member of the team launching Operation Valkyrie.

Just before 11 o'clock on the morning of 20 July, Stauffenberg and his assistant, Lieutenant Werner von Haeften, drove through the final series of checkpoint barriers and into the inner compound of armoured huts and concrete bunkers. This was 'the Wolf's Lair' – Hitler's heavily guarded hiding place, from which he led the campaigns and battles of the last months of the war in Europe.

❖   ❖   ❖

The conference with Hitler was scheduled for 12.30. Fifteen minutes before, Stauffenberg made his excuses and asked to change his shirt. It was an unpleasantly hot and sticky day. His request did not seem strange, especially as he was shortly to meet the leader of Germany. He was shown to a washroom and then a waiting room and was relieved to see no one follow him inside.

Moments later, his assistant, Haeften, joined him, and they quickly began to activate the two bombs. A small tube containing acid had to be broken open. The acid would take around ten minutes to eat through a thin, steel wire. When this wire broke, it would set off the bomb's detonator and its three-quarters of a kilo of explosives.

Stauffenberg gripped his special pliers with his three fingers and used the tool to break the acid fuse tube on one of the bombs. Before the second bomb could be activated, a German soldier entered the room. He announced that the conference with Hitler had begun. Stauffenberg and Haeften had only just managed to hide what they were doing.

Carrying just the one activated bomb, Stauffenberg made his way over to the meeting place. Twice on the way, he was asked by a German officer if he would like help with his briefcase. Twice he refused. He hid his dismay when he saw that, instead of Hitler's regular bunker, made of concrete, the meeting was being held in a large wooden hut with three windows. This building would not contain the blast well, making the bomb less effective, but still Stauffenberg continued. There was no turning back now. The bomb had less than eight minutes before it would detonate.

❖ ❖ ❖

Stauffenberg entered the hut and asked to stand near Hitler so that his damaged hearing could pick up everything the leader said. Field Marshal Keitel, an avid supporter of Hitler, was annoyed with Stauffenberg for being late. If Hitler was irritated, he didn't show it. He wordlessly shook Stauffenberg's left hand. Many of the senior German officers present knew that Hitler admired Stauffenberg's bravery and intelligence.

Stauffenberg was shown to a seat two places along from Hitler. He tried to edge closer to his target but he knew that time was running out and any further requests or strange movements might arouse suspicion. He carefully placed his briefcase as close to Hitler as he could.

Stauffenberg's heart leapt into his mouth when Field Marshal Keitel indicated that he should give his report next. This would be disastrous, as there was now no more than six minutes before the bomb went off. He had assumed that his report would be required later in the meeting. Stauffenberg stalled for a moment, long enough for a discussion about the war with Russia to start.

With time running out, Stauffenberg knew he had to escape the hut. He mumbled something about an urgent phone call from his headquarters at Berlin and briskly walked out. Field Marshal Keitel was furious with him. How dare he show so little respect to his senior officers? But Hitler let him leave. Everything was now in place.

❖   ❖   ❖

Stauffenberg hurried over to another hut where he was greeted by the Chief of Signals at Hitler's base. He, too, was in on the plot. Both men waited tensely as the seconds crawled by.

As soon as the explosion sounded, Stauffenberg's assistant, Werner von Haeften, slammed his foot down on the accelerator of the staff car he was driving and sped over to collect Stauffenberg. They drove on through the checkpoints at the base. Despite the confusion following the explosion, the well-known war hero, Colonel Stauffenberg, with the patch over his eye and the missing hand, was easily recognized. Soon they had left the Wolf's Lair and were at the airfield, where a specially prepared Heinkel 111 plane was waiting to ferry the two men back to headquarters in Berlin.

For more than three hours, as he journeyed through the air and then, by road, to Berlin, Stauffenberg was cut off from all that was happening – or not happening as it turned out. General Olbricht, the leader of the conspiracy, was unsure whether Hitler was alive or dead. He delayed putting Operation Valkyrie into action until Stauffenberg arrived.

Meanwhile, despite being told of the overthrow attempt by Olbricht, General Fromm still refused to go along with it and was locked away. When Stauffenberg arrived at the War Ministry, he tried to make the General change his mind but to no avail. Operation Valkyrie was launched but – without Fromm's authority and his voice giving orders on the phone – officers in other parts of Germany wavered.

❖ ❖ ❖

Back at Hitler's base, the hut had been demolished, yet – amazingly – only four of the twenty-four people present were killed. Hitler's clothing was in tatters, his hair singed, his eardrum ruptured and he had a sprained elbow. But he was alive and able to speak and issue commands.

The discussion about the war with Russia had continued after Stauffenberg had left the hut. One of the officers, Colonel Brandt, had leaned forward to make sure he heard something Hitler said when his foot had bumped into the lethal briefcase. Brandt had picked the case up and moved it away from the table and Hitler. This extra slice of bad luck for the conspirators saved Hitler's life.

Hitler and his loyal generals launched a speedy investigation in which it became clear that Stauffenberg had placed the bomb. Throughout the afternoon and evening, the Home Army did take control of some key places but the conspirators were not ruthless enough in eliminating opponents. Those loyal to Hitler still kept control of many important facilities such as radio stations. It was from one such station in Berlin that news emerged that Hitler had survived the assassination attempt. German soldiers and officers were confused. What was going on?

❖ ❖ ❖

By that night, the War Ministry in Berlin was surrounded by those loyal to Hitler. It appeared to be only a matter of time before the conspirators would be caught. Yet Stauffenberg refused to give in and insisted there was still a chance. He cajoled his colleagues and tried to raise spirits. But, deep within the War Ministry building itself, a small group of Nazi officers, loyal to Hitler, had armed themselves and fought to capture the conspirators.

They burst into Olbricht's office with guns at the ready. Stauffenberg entered the room seconds later and was greeted with a volley of machine-gun fire. One bullet lodged in his upper arm. General Fromm had been released and strode into the office. It was over. The conspiracy had failed. Stauffenberg's uniform was drenched in blood. Yet, even then, in great pain, he refused to implicate any of the others. He insisted it was all his own idea and that he had forced his fellow officers to carry out his orders.

Of course, Fromm had known about the plot, even though he had refused to co-operate with the conspirators. But he now had to cover his own tracks and show himself to be completely behind Hitler. The brutal torture techniques used by the Gestapo (the German secret police) were legendary. Men and women would be systematically abused until they just hung on to life, yet could tolerate no more agony. Even men as gallant and brave as Stauffenberg, Olbricht and their assistants would eventually break under such torture, Fromm believed. He did not want to take the risk of being named, and therefore sentenced Stauffenberg, Haeften, Olbricht and Olbricht's assistant, Colonel Mertz von Quirnhem, to immediate execution.

Others protested. Surely they should wait until the Gestapo arrived? But Fromm would not hear of it. The four were marched out into the murky darkness of the courtyard at the back of the ministry buildings. Stauffenberg was bleeding badly from his wound but seemed unconcerned. It was just after midnight and the four conspirators remained calm, as a staff car's headlights were powered up.

The four were to be executed in order of rank. Olbricht was shot first. Then it was Stauffenberg's turn. He calmly stood and awaited his fate. As the firing squad took aim, Haeften, loyal to the very last, threw himself in front of his commander to try to save him. The gesture proved futile. Stauffenberg shouted, 'Long live our sacred Germany' as he was cut down by a hail of bullets.

Fromm planned to execute more conspirators but the arrival of the Gestapo prevented him from doing so. The Gestapo wanted as many as possible taken alive. For the rest of the war, right up until the very last days before Germany surrendered, the Gestapo and the Schutzstaffel (SS), Hitler's personal bodyguard, were occupied in investigating possible conspirators. Over 7,000 people were arrested. But Stauffenberg's refusal to name names is believed to have saved the lives of dozens of soldiers involved in the overthrow attempt.

The conspiracy had been long in the planning and well thought out but, on the day of its launch, three pieces of bad luck had sealed its failure. If the meeting with Hitler had been held in the usual bunker, if Stauffenberg and Haeften had been able to arm both bombs, and if an impatient Colonel Brandt hadn't moved the bag so as to get a better look at the campaign maps, the whole endeavour might have gone very differently – and many, many lives might have been saved.

We will never know what the outcome would have been if Stauffenberg and the others had secured power. But history tells us that he was a brilliant and brave soldier who fought hard for his country until he could no longer tolerate the ways of the Nazis, especially their leader. Stauffenberg had been prepared to sacrifice his own life in order to take Germany in a new direction, and put an end to the senseless killing.

◆ ◆ ◆

CHAPTER 4

The Dambusters

The war in Europe was partly a test of both sides' industrial might. Millions of workers were employed making military vehicles and weapons to be used in the conflict.

In Germany, the Ruhr Valley was the site of a great many industrial plants. The plants received their water supply, and much of their electricity (via hydro-electric power), from massive dams, which also protected them from flooding. In 1938, a year before the war started, the British Air Ministry had targeted these dams. Destroying them would be a major blow to Germany. But how could it be done? The answer lay in the brainwork of a famous aero-engineer and the flying skill and heroism of a group of men forever remembered as the Dambusters.

◆　◆　◆

It stood at the far end of the Moehne Lake. Made of limestone rubble masonry and over half a kilometre long, the Moehne Dam was almost 40 metres thick at its base. In the night gloom, it looked huge and very, very solid.

'God!' exclaimed one of the British crew of the eight low-flying Lancaster bombers, 'Can we break that?'

No one dared answer. Certainly, regular bombs, even the largest the Royal Air Force (RAF) possessed, wouldn't make a dent in the massive construction. The dam was guarded by nets strung across the water to stop underwater attacks. But these Lancasters from the newly formed 617 Squadron were equipped with an ingenious new weapon designed by the famous aero-engineer, Barnes Wallis.

Led by Wing Commander Guy Gibson, the planes wheeled away from the lake and took stock of the situation. They were the first wave of aircraft, nine in total, which had taken off from the east coast of England at around 8.30 p.m. on 16 May 1943. Two further waves would be attacking other dams in the area.

Flying at incredibly low altitudes, below 160 metres, the Lancasters had crossed the North Sea and Holland and crept silently into Germany. The crews were forbidden to use their radios in case the enemy picked up their signals. Yet, despite these precautions, the formation had already lost one of their number; Lancaster AJ-B piloted by Flight Lieutenant Astell had been shot down by heavy fire from guns on the ground. Could eight aircraft, each equipped with just one bomb, destroy the mighty structure ahead of them? The air crew's leader, Guy Gibson, thought so.

❖   ❖   ❖

Gibson had been rejected once from the RAF on account of being too short for flying service but managed to get in at his second attempt. He trained hard and became famous as a skilled pilot, a strict commander and a man with an intense love of flying. His office at the airfield was even painted sky blue, with aeroplanes and birds daubed on the walls. At the age of just twenty-four, he had already flown 170 fighter and bomber missions and been highly decorated.

Gibson was told to hand-pick 130 members of a new, top-secret bomber group, first known as X Squadron and then 617 Squadron. The unit was formed in March 1943 and was based at RAF

Scampton in Lincolnshire. They were a mixed group. Some were veterans of low-flying missions, others had relatively little experience, but all were considered by Gibson to have the 'right stuff' – the nerve and skill to carry out what was still a completely unknown mission. The 133 members of 617 Squadron included twenty-nine Canadians, twelve Australians, two New Zealanders and an American, Flight Lieutenant Joe McCarthy.

All the men of 617 Squadron trained intensively using Avro Lancaster bombers, which were among the best Allied heavy bombers of World War II. Powered by four reliable Rolls Royce Merlin engines (the same as those used in the Spitfire fighter), the Lancaster was a tough, robust aircraft, well-liked by those who flew it. Lancasters were designed to bomb from heights of over 6,000 metres. Anything below 300 or 400 metres was considered dangerous.

Yet, when the crews for this mission started their training, they had to fly at just 80 metres above the ground or water. When they got used to that, the height was reduced to between 40 and 50 metres and they were sent out at night.

What mission would require this sort of flying? Many of the crews thought they would be bombing German battleships but eventually they were shown their specially modified Lancasters, designed to hold a quite different sort of weapon. It was officially called Upkeep, but is better known as Barnes Wallis's 'bouncing bomb'.

❖ ❖ ❖

At first glance, Upkeep looked like a large, apparently harmless barrel about 1.5 metres in length. The commander in charge of 617 and other squadrons, Air Vice Marshal Cochrane, described it as a 'lump of iron resembling a large garden roller'. But it was about as heavy as three family cars, and nearly two-thirds of its weight was taken up by a deadly explosive called Torpex.

Barnes Wallis had come up with the idea of a bouncing bomb by watching pebbles skimming across flat stretches of water. He tried out his idea using marbles over a tin bath full of water, and then using small, spinning balls and cylinders in a testing centre's water tank. Full-sized prototypes were built and tested. The bouncing bomb looked as if it could work in theory, but it demanded a great deal from the flight crews.

The 'bomb in a barrel' rested on a special frame which included a motor. Before being dropped, the motor would spin the bomb so that it turned around 500 times per minute. If released at a height of just under 20 metres, when the aircraft was flying at just over 240 kilometres per hour, it would skim across the lake, avoiding any torpedo nets, and come to rest against the dam wall. With no more forward speed to keep it above water, the heavy bomb would quickly sink. At a depth of about 9 metres, it would explode, right up against the dam wall.

On the final training runs the crews had to practise with dummy bombs at under 30 metres. At this terrifying, ground-scraping altitude, even the slightest misjudgement would prove lethal. There was no spare height to correct a mistake. It is a tribute to 617's flying skill that no aircraft were lost during these training flights.

❖ ❖ ❖

Now, having flown for almost three and a half hours, and with their target looming ahead, it was time to put their training into practice. Gibson would go first, as planned. He pulled his aircraft around, checked his crew were ready and dived down towards the lake. Levelling out mere metres above the water's surface, he checked the two specially fitted spotlights as they lit up small circles of the water. When they crossed exactly, then the plane was flying at the right height.

As Gibson steered the Lancaster, the ten or so German gunners on top of the dam started to let rip with their powerful anti-aircraft guns. The air lit up like a deadly firework display, with the red and yellow lights of tracer bullets heading towards Gibson's aircraft. Gibson timed his approach to the dam wall. Apart from being released at an exact height and speed, the bomb also had to be dropped – according to Barnes Wallis's calculations – just over 390 metres from the target. Under heavy enemy fire, he gave the signal, the bomb was dropped and the aircraft pulled away from the scene. The bomb exploded to the side of the dam, appearing to do little important damage.

Now the second Lancaster entered the danger zone to make its approach run. The enemy fire grew even more intense and the aircraft was hit several times. Its bomb was released but missed the target, and Gibson and the other Lancasters were sickened as they saw their comrade's plane crash and burst into flames nearby.

❖   ❖   ❖

Gibson feared they would have further losses, especially those who had to attack after him – without the advantage of surprise. Piloting his plane back over the dam, he hoped to draw the gunners' fire away from the incoming bombers and try to knock out some of the anti-aircraft fire with his plane's own machine guns.

The third and then the fourth Lancaster flew in low and fast, attempting to destroy the massive structure. Both planes dropped their bombs which skimmed across the water and exploded, as planned. The fourth run looked perfect – a water spout right next to the dam, and over 300 metres high, exploded into the night sky. Yet the dam still stood.

For the fifth and final attempt on the Moehne Dam, Gibson changed things around. He and another Lancaster flew alongside, hoping to knock out more of the enemy's fire and also to act as targets, distracting the Germans from the armed aircraft. As the three approached, their turrets blazed machine-gun fire at the defending gun positions. The bomb was released and skipped four times across the water before sinking and exploding.

Most of the flak from the anti-aircraft guns had stopped; and the gun batteries had been silenced, destroyed by machine-gun fire from the turrets on the Lancasters. Circling above the lake, Gibson and the crews of the surviving Lancasters watched in awe as a central section of the Moehne Dam started to crumble and fall away.

A vast and powerful surge of water swelled up over the broken dam; then giant wave after wave rolled down, flooding the valley. In his own words,

Gibson said: 'We began to shout and scream and act like madmen over the R/T [radio transmitter] for this was a tremendous sight, a sight which probably no man will ever see again.'

❖ ❖ ❖

But Gibson and some of the others still had work to do. Five aircraft flew on to the Eder Dam, shrouded in early morning mist. Just three Lancasters had bouncing bombs left to attempt to destroy the 40 metre high, 400 metre long dam. The fog caused many problems.

The first two Lancasters flew in and released their bombs. The first bomb was bang on target but didn't destroy the dam. The second was released a little late, crashed into the top of the barrier and flew over. Both bombs exploded, sending up huge fountains of water but failing to breach the dam. Flying above the scene, Gibson watched in dismay. There was one Lancaster bomber left with a bomb. It was piloted by a quiet young Australian, Pilot Officer L.G. Knight.

Knight and the six crew members of Lancaster AJ-N were their last chance. Gibson and the others could only hope that the first two explosions had weakened the dam enough, and that Knight's flying would be totally accurate. Knight carefully piloted his Lancaster down on the right line along the lake.

The lake was eerily dark and at such low levels it was very hard to judge distances correctly. Knight pulled out of his first run; he hadn't got his positioning right. He tried a second time and again couldn't get on to the correct line. Pulling away from the dam, he received lots of encouragement from his crew. They all knew how hard the manoeuvre was.

Knight dived again and levelled out just above the lake. The six crew members manned their stations tensely and watched as the bomb dropped and then skipped across the water. As they pulled away, there was a tremendous explosion. The Eder Dam had been breached! Immediately, 200 million tonnes of water started to pour through the dam, but the noise of the rushing water could barely be heard above the wild celebrations inside the bomber plane.

By the time they touched down at their base in RAF Scampton, the mood aboard the returning Lancasters was much more serious. They had lost two further aircraft – shot down by the Germans – as they headed back after their attack on the dams. Of the first wave of nine aircraft, only five got home safely.

The second and third waves of Lancasters, sent

to attack the Sorpe and Ennepe Dams, fared just as badly. The second wave had one bomber damaged by flak and two shot down. Another aircraft had to turn back, leaving only one bomber to attempt to destroy the Sorpe Dam. The plane's crew risked everything and managed to drop their bomb but did not breach its wall. Only two of the five aircraft in the third wave reached their targets. They attacked the Sorpe and Ennepe Dams but, again, without success.

Although those who made it back to base were elated at the partial success of their daring raid, there was much sadness at the loss of so many of their comrades. The empty chairs in the squadron's canteen and dining area, known as the mess, were a heart-breaking sight. Fifty-six men did not return from the dambusting raid. Fifty-three were killed in action, while the other three were captured and became prisoners of war.

Barnes Wallis wept at the news of so many deaths and came to regret having invented the device. 'All those boys. All those boys,' he lamented.

The day after the dams raid, a photo-reconnaissance aircraft flew over the dams and the surrounding area. The resulting photographs showed that two dams had been seriously damaged.

The breach in the top part of the Moehne Dam, reported by Gibson, turned out to be over 130 metres long.

Gibson was awarded the Victoria Cross to go with his earlier medals, the Distinguished Service Order (DSO) and bar and the Distinguished Service Cross (DSC). Only one British flyer, Leonard Cheshire, was as highly decorated as the young leader of 617 Squadron. A total of thirty-four decorations were awarded to members of the 16 May raid and the squadron was highly commended.

❖ ❖ ❖

On 19 September 1944, Guy Gibson was flying a Mosquito aircraft, on a mission to bomb some railway yards not far from the Dutch town of Steenbergen. The Mosquito was quite unlike the Lancaster bomber which Gibson had piloted during his most famous raid; it was light, fast and carried just two people, Gibson and his navigator, Squadron Leader Jim Warwick. For reasons which remain a mystery, the pair did not return. Witnesses saw the aircraft trailing flames before it crashed in a field. The plane may have been shot down or the engine may have failed. But, whatever the cause, both men were killed.

Gibson's memoirs, entitled Enemy Coast Ahead, were published after his death, in 1946. He vividly described the training for the raid and the raid itself, and the book became a bestseller. Other books on the bouncing bomb and the squadron who flew with it were published and a major movie on the subject was released. Even today, 617 Squadron, now flying Panavia Tornado swing-wing jets, is still known as 'the dambusting squadron'.

❖ ❖ ❖

Yet, despite the mission's fame, many military historians have questioned its real value. The loss of life was high, and the breached Moehne Dam was repaired within months, although its power station was never rebuilt. Electricity and other supplies were brought in from other parts of the country, and the Moehne and Sorpe Dams remained standing.

On the other hand, Germany had to divert large resources to repair the damage, and there was a great loss of equipment and transport links such as bridges. Roughly 10,000 troops and large amounts of military hardware were sent to protect the dams, drawing vital forces away from other parts of Germany.

Meanwhile, in Britain, the mission certainly succeeded in boosting the nation's morale. The British government promoted it as a great triumph for RAF's Bomber Command and a tribute to the co-operation between air crews from a number of different countries. The debate on the raid's impact rages on to this day. But what has never been in doubt is the bravery and extreme skill shown by the crews of 617 Squadron who dared to attack Germany's mighty dams with a bomb inspired by a pebble.

◆ ◆ ◆

CHAPTER 5

Shipwrecked!

The USA entered World War II after the Japanese bombed Pearl Harbour in December 1941. American troops fought the Japanese in the Pacific – on the land, and in the air space and waters of the world's largest ocean.

Deep in the South Pacific (almost as far south as the northern coast of Australia), lie the Solomon Islands. Thirteen crewmen were thought to have perished there in August 1943, when the US Navy gunboat *PT109* was sunk by a Japanese destroyer. But all was not lost, thanks to the extraordinary courage and endurance of the boat's skipper, John F. Kennedy (later to become US president). Largely due to his bravery, eleven of their number were rescued and managed to survive for a week in incredibly hostile conditions.

❖   ❖   ❖

The US Navy motor torpedo boat, *PT109*, headed at full speed towards the dock. Its skipper waited until the very last moment before giving the signal to reverse the engines on full power. The 25 metre long boat's three big engines suddenly died. *PT109* now had no brakes. Dock workers fled out of the way as the boat crashed into the pier. Its crew were knocked to the floor but luckily no one was hurt. From that day on, the skipper, a young, junior lieutenant called John Fitzgerald Kennedy, was known as 'Crash' by the other American servicemen stationed at the Russell Islands, part of a bigger South Pacific island chain called the Solomon Islands.

Kennedy had been cruising back from a routine patrol when his competitive streak had forced him into a race with another American gunboat. Kennedy escaped with nothing more serious than a severe telling-off. It was the summer of 1943, and discipline in the squadrons of PT boats patrolling the waters around the South Pacific islands was a little more relaxed than in other services.

Six months earlier, Kennedy had been bored and fretting to see some action. He had been stationed in Panama, Central America, a long way from any combat zone. Strictly speaking, he shouldn't have been accepted into the Navy at all, as he suffered from a bad back and other ailments. Yet his determination to contribute to the war effort had seen him through training and then, having begged for a transfer, to where the real action was. At the end of April 1943, Kennedy was posted to the South Pacific, where he took charge of a gunboat, *PT109*.

From their bases, PT boats conducted nightly attacks on Japanese convoys of warships and barges which were carrying reinforcements and supplies to Japanese troops on neighbouring islands. It was on one of these operations that Kennedy and his crew of twelve set out on the evening of 1 August. Kennedy's friend, Barney Ross, whose own PT boat had been sunk, joined the mission and was appointed lookout. *PT109* was stationed at the back of the fifteen-boat task force, and there was no radio contact between the boats.

The night was pitch black with few stars to be seen. It remained eerily dark and quiet as the boat cruised through the Solomon Islands, on the hunt for Japanese vessels. *PT109* was running on only one of its engines to reduce its wake (the tell-tale pattern of water behind it), which Japanese bomber planes would search for, to launch their bombs.

Suddenly, a shout went up: 'Ship at 2 o'clock!'

The ship was a Japanese destroyer, the *Amagiri*, sailing very fast – over 30 knots. Kennedy sounded battle stations and spun the wheel hard. But, powered by just one engine, *PT109* responded sluggishly. In moments, the *Amagiri* was upon *PT109*.

CRASH!

The accident at the dock a few weeks earlier was a tiny bump compared to this. The Japanese destroyer, with its thick metal armour plating, cut right through the wooden hull of the American gunboat. The majority of the crew of the *Amagiri* didn't even feel the impact and weren't aware that they had sliced through another craft. But Kennedy was thrown on to his bad back by the force of the collision. So this is how it feels to be killed, he thought, as he lay on the floor and saw the hull of the Japanese destroyer tear through the boat he commanded.

❖ ❖ ❖

Most of the crew were above decks and many were thrown into the water by the crash. One man, Pat 'Pop' MacMahon, was in the engine room when a fireball engulfed the cramped compartment. As water poured in, the terrified MacMahon splashed as hard as he could to try to keep a ring of water between him and the flames.

The *Amagiri* ploughed onwards and away from *PT109* into the murky darkness, leaving devastation behind. The torpedo boat was practically destroyed. Only a large chunk of its hull, containing several watertight compartments, remained intact and afloat. Dazed and in pain, Kennedy was more concerned for his crew than himself. He yelled out for signs of life among the wreckage.

Eleven out of the thirteen crew responded. Two men, Andrew Kirksey and Harold Marney, went down with part of the boat. It's believed that they died instantly at the time of the collision. MacMahon was still alive but had suffered terrible burns. Other crew members had broken or sprained limbs, or had inhaled fumes from the burning fuel and were struggling to breathe. Several of the crew forced into the sea couldn't swim and were fighting to keep their heads above water.

Quick action was needed. Kennedy, Ross and Kennedy's second-in-command, Lenny Thom, found and rescued those who couldn't swim. Clinging on to what remained of their boat, the crew of *PT109* thanked God for sparing their lives. Then they lay and waited. News of their accident would surely filter back to their base and a search party would be sent out.

❖　❖　❖

Night turned to day and there was still no sign of any friendly plane or boat on the horizon. Around 10 in the morning, the floating part of *PT109* started to lurch badly. It was clear that it would sink soon. Most of the sailors had been in the water for eight hours now. They had to find land. Four islands could be viewed from the wreck. The largest, Kolombangara Island, was known to hold 10,000 Japanese troops. The next two closest, Gizo and Vella Lavella, were also teeming with Japanese soldiers. There was only one choice. To the southeast, about 5 kilometres away, lay a group of small islands. Kennedy told his men they would have to swim for it.

Those who could not swim well held on tightly to a large piece of timber from the wreck of the *PT109*. This still left poor MacMahon, badly burned and barely conscious. Kennedy declared he would look after MacMahon while the others looked after those who could swim but were injured and those who could not swim at all.

With the long strap of MacMahon's lifejacket held between his gritted teeth, Kennedy started his slow, tortuous journey. Fortunately, he had been on the swimming team during his student days at Harvard University; now he needed every ounce of the skill and strength he'd developed. Swimming breaststroke, and with his back aching from the collision, Kennedy forced himself through the water, pulling the other man's heavy body behind him.

Onwards and onwards, Kennedy and the others slowly swam. There were sharks in the water which swam perilously close to them on several occasions. Kennedy and his men were also fearful of being spotted and attacked by the Japanese troops on the other islands. Their fear drove them on through the ocean currents with the harsh sun beating down.

❖　❖　❖

Nearly five hours later, Kennedy collapsed on the edge of the tiny island, completely exhausted. He had been in the water for over fifteen hours and his stomach was cramping from all the seawater he had swallowed. The surviving crew of the *PT109* had all reached land, but their island refuge was less than 50 metres in diameter. There was no one around and no drinkable water. The crew protected themselves from the hot sun by hiding in the bushes and the small grove of trees in the centre of the island.

Later that day, Kennedy went off in search of rescue or, at least, a more suitable refuge. Swimming round the edge of the island, he was soon out in deep water. He had a signals pistol with him which could fire a flare; and he hoped to use it as a rescue signal should he encounter a friendly boat.

Treading water through much of the night, Kennedy had no luck and started wearily back to the others. But he had underestimated his own tiredness and the strength of the current. He struggled to make headway and began to lose consciousness. Still out in deep water, with his energy waning, Kennedy again felt that he was about to die. His mind drifted off into a hazy, half-sleep as he let himself be carried by the swirls of the ocean waves. There was nothing more he could do.

Back on the island, the crew's morale had dipped. Kennedy had been gone for too long. Some felt they were doomed, and all were exhausted and suffering from extreme thirst. Kennedy's second-in-command, Lenny Thom, tried to keep everyone's spirits up, first cracking jokes and then generating arguments to keep the men alert. They had tried to lick water off the leaves of trees and bushes but found them all covered with bird droppings. The crew nicknamed the place 'Bird Island'.

The currents that flow around Bird Island and the other Solomon Islands change direction frequently. Incredibly, the semi-conscious Kennedy floated past Bird Island, past the Japanese strongholds of Gizo and Kolombangara, and back almost to where he had started.

When he came to, many hours later, he assumed he had just dreamed what had happened before. But the cold water and his aches and pains were real enough. Slowly, Kennedy dredged up enough strength to make his way back to the shore. It was light by the time he fell on to the beach and was violently sick. The crew were overjoyed to see him, although he looked terribly weak. They helped him to some shade where he slept.

The next night, Barney Ross tried the same journey as Kennedy. He had not gone far when the strong currents overwhelmed him. Having managed to turn back just in time to avoid a large school of sand sharks, he returned to the others with the news that he had lost the crew's only lantern on the journey.

It was obvious to the survivors that they could

not stay on Bird Island for much longer. Kennedy decided that they should all journey on to a slightly larger island, on which he thought he had seen palm trees holding coconuts. It would be risky to move the most injured men, but the only alternative would be to stay on Bird Island and slowly die of thirst and hunger.

Again, Kennedy towed MacMahon through the water, using his teeth to grip the lifejacket strap. They reached Olasana Island and feasted greedily on coconuts; too greedily in many cases, as most of them were sick from suddenly taking in too much of the sweet milk and coconut flesh.

❖ ❖ ❖

Despite now having some food and liquid, the crew's spirits were getting lower and lower. MacMahon's dirt-covered burns had become infected, and it wasn't clear how much longer he could survive. The rest of the crew didn't dare say it but they knew that the lack of boats and planes in the area was ominous. No one was out searching for them. They were genuinely shipwrecked on a desert island; and, with each passing day, their chances of being rescued appeared to shrink.

Kennedy, however, refused to admit defeat and asked Ross to swim with him to an island called Nauru (now known as Naru). A stretch of sea,

Ferguson's Passage, lay to the far side of the island, and Kennedy knew that American boats sometimes patrolled there.

Compared with their other swims, the journey to Nauru was short and uneventful. An hour after they set off, they reached its shores and started to explore. No ships could be seen in Ferguson's Passage but, just as even Kennedy's determination started to waver, fortune smiled upon them. They chanced upon two native islanders. Both pairs of men were wary of each other at first and neither could speak each other's language. Kennedy and Ross had to work hard to convince them that they were not Japanese. But once this was proved, the islanders became friendly.

The islanders had no room in their own canoe to rescue Kennedy and Ross, let alone the others still on Olasana Island. Instead, they led Kennedy and Ross to a small, battered canoe made from a hollowed-out tree trunk.

Kennedy and Ross desperately needed to get a message back to an Allied base. They had no paper or way of writing upon leaves but one of the islanders had the answer. Scrambling up a tree, he fetched down a coconut. Kennedy still had his pocket knife with him. He carefully scratched a message on the shell of the coconut. It read: 'NAURO ISL NATIVE KNOWS POSIT HE CAN

PILOT 11 ALIVE NEED SMALL BOAT KENNEDY.'

Kennedy figured that the nearest American base was at Rendova and repeated this word to the islanders over and over again. The islanders took Kennedy's message and paddled off. Kennedy and Ross were elated but knew they were not saved yet. To get to Rendova, the islanders had to paddle through enemy waters. If the message was found by the Japanese, the shipwreck survivors might be attacked or left to die. Even if the islanders completed their journey, there was no guarantee that their message would be believed.

❖   ❖   ❖

For the rest of the day, Kennedy and Ross lay in the shade. They both had fevers and were famished and dizzy with thirst. That evening, still feverish, Kennedy came round enough to attempt one more trip. Ross thought the sea looked too rough for their small, low-lying canoe, but Kennedy insisted.

Out the two went into the waters of Ferguson Passage, hoping to spot a passing American patrol boat. They had only been paddling for a few minutes when the wind increased. The waves got higher and higher until they were 2 metres tall and were swamping the tiny dugout canoe.

Soon the tiny craft was being carried back towards a deadly coral reef. There was nothing they could do except hold on for dear life and pray. A massive wave tore Kennedy's hands from the side of the canoe. He was swept up into the churning waters and spun over and over. Pain from the coral cutting into his body told Kennedy that he had been dashed on to the reef. For the third time in just a few days, he thought he was about to die. Suddenly, his feet touched the bottom. His head emerged above the surface and he spat out seawater.

'Barney! Barney Ross!' Kennedy shouted. There was no reply. Standing up slowly, battered and bruised, Kennedy again shouted out to his friend. This time Ross answered. He, too, had been thrown on to the reef and his feet had been badly sliced by its sharp edges. The two waded, slowly and painfully, through the reef and on to dry land.

Exhausted and in pain, the two friends collapsed on the shore of Nauru Island. Although Kennedy wouldn't admit it, he was beginning to lose hope. Would they ever be saved? The pair fell into a troubled sleep.

❖ ❖ ❖

Ross and Kennedy were woken on 7 August by a canoe carrying eight native islanders. Kennedy and Ross were both scared until their leader, Benjamin Kevu, spoke. In perfect English, he said: 'I have a letter for you, sir.' Kennedy couldn't believe it. The two islanders had delivered the coconut successfully and the letter in reply was from an officer at a New Zealand coastwatching camp on Komu Island.

The letter urged Kennedy to come back with the islanders to the New Zealand base, as both American and New Zealand commanders feared that the message might be a Japanese hoax. After all, the boat had been sunk in hostile waters and the crew had been missing for almost a week. How could they have survived?

Kennedy agreed, but first the islanders transported Ross and Kennedy back to deliver supplies of food and water to the rest of *PT109*'s crew on Olasana Island. Kennedy then travelled to the New Zealand base. He spent the entire journey hidden in the bottom of the islanders' canoe, covered by giant palm tree leaves. It was vital for him to remain hidden, as a number of Japanese aircraft flew low over the boat to take a close look. They did not detect its secret cargo.

Kennedy was welcomed warmly by the New Zealanders and plans were made to carry out a rescue. Although at the very limits of his endurance, Kennedy was desperate to see his men safe.

The next evening, under cover of darkness, the

PT157 carried out its rescue mission. Kennedy was aboard, and when the US Navy craft arrived at Olasana Island he hugged each of his men as they limped or were carried on. All those who survived the initial destruction of the *PT109* had made it through their eight-day ordeal.

❖   ❖   ❖

Despite his injuries, Kennedy took command of another PT boat only a month after his safe return. He had to return to hospital to have his back treated the following year, and it was while he was in hospital that he received the US Navy and Marine Corps medal.

His citation read:

'For heroism in the rescue of three men following the ramming and sinking of his motor torpedo boat while attempting a torpedo attack on a Japanese destroyer in the Solomon Islands area on the night of Aug 1-2, 1943. Lt. KENNEDY, Capt. of the boat, directed the rescue of the crew and personally rescued 3 men, one of whom was seriously injured. During the following 6 days, he succeeded in getting his crew ashore, and after swimming many hours attempting to secure aid and food, finally effected the rescue of the men. His courage, endurance and excellent leadership contributed to the saving of several lives and was in keeping with the highest traditions of the United States Naval Service.'

❖   ❖   ❖

Kennedy himself was always quick to point out that there had been eleven heroes, not just one. All the crew had showed incredible determination to survive, and Kennedy remained modest about his wartime bravery. When a little boy asked him, years later, how he became a hero, he answered, 'I had no choice – they sunk my boat.'

In 1960, John F. Kennedy, now known as 'Jack' rather than 'Crash', became the thirty-fifth president of the United States. Before his untimely death – when he was assassinated in Dallas, Texas, in 1963 – President Kennedy met up with the surviving members of his crew and was toasted by crew members of the *Amagiri*.

◆   ◆   ◆

CHAPTER 6

By the Skin of His Teeth

Britain's Royal Air Force fighter pilots played a central part in the early stages of World War II. Just a few months after helping to evacuate Allied troops from Dunkirk in 1940, the RAF fought one of the most important campaigns of the entire war – the Battle of Britain. Including British, Australian, Canadian, New Zealand, Dutch and Polish airmen in its ranks, the RAF suffered massive losses but just managed to win the vital battle for air supremacy.

The bravery of 'the few' – the pilots of the Spitfire and Hurricane fighter planes – in repelling the mighty Luftwaffe was a major turning point in the war. Without question, the fighter pilots operated as a close-knit team. But some, whether through luck, skill or daring, became particularly famous for their exploits. Among them was a man who had come within a whisker of dying in a mid-air collision in 1938, Roland Robert Stanford Tuck.

◆　◆　◆

Attack! The German Messerschmitt Me109s came from above and behind the Spitfires of 92 Squadron. It was late May 1940, and the planes of 92 Squadron, led by Roger Bushell, were patrolling the skies above Dunkirk. Down below them, the huge evacuation of Allied troops and equipment back across the English Channel had just started.

The Spitfire and Me109 fighter planes were extremely well-matched. The Spitfire was easier to manoeuvre in the air but the Messerschmitt was a little faster. Me109s and Spitfires were involved in hundreds of dogfights in the air space above southern England throughout the late spring and summer of 1940, in the lead-up to the Battle of Britain.

As 92 Squadron was attacked from above and behind, Roland Tuck was pleased to see some action at last, and wheeled his Spitfire into combat. His squadron broke from their tight formation and Tuck immediately spotted a lone Me109. He pulled his nimble craft around the sky, seeking his target, and opened fire from a distance of around 450 metres. His machine-gun bullets struck the enemy aircraft's wing, tearing it to pieces.

Tuck watched with grim satisfaction as the Me109 lost height and started to spiral towards the ground. He followed the stricken enemy fighter down until he was sure it would not be returning to combat. Then the British pilot headed back to join his squadron.

After returning to their base at Hornchurch, in the south of England, Tuck and the others set off on another patrol over Dunkirk a little later that day. This time, the small squadron of British planes attacked around thirty Messerschmitt Me110 fighters. Although these two-seater German aircraft featured a rear gunner, they were slower and less manouverable than the Me109s and Tuck managed to shoot two down. In his first day's combat, Stanford Tuck had shot down three enemy aircraft. Not bad for a man who had nearly failed his pilot's training a few years earlier.

Tuck had originally joined the Merchant Navy in search of action and adventure. He enjoyed the time he spent on board ship, travelling the world. But, while he was home in Catford, in south-east London, on a few days leave, a newspaper advert caught his eye. 'Fly with the RAF!' it urged, and Tuck's imagination was well and truly captured.

The young man passed the written, oral and medical examinations and began pilot training. There was only one problem – he appeared to have no natural ability to fly aeroplanes. He fumbled with the controls and was dangerously heavy-handed. When a slight tilt was required to adjust the plane's flying position, Tuck would over-enthusiastically yank the controls this way and that. He was desperate to succeed and never relaxed in the training cockpit.

The instructors started to despair of him. They liked the enthusiastic, ex-seaman who was a brilliant shot – the result of both his father teaching him how to shoot a gun as a youngster and the time he had spent on board ship shooting fish and sharks with an old rifle. But they, like Tuck, could not see how he would pass his solo flights.

As Tuck pulled off the ground on his now-or-never solo test flight in 1935, he felt he had no chance of succeeding. But then, suddenly, the pressure was off and he found himself relaxed in an aircraft cockpit for the first time. The instructors were amazed. He still had some work to do, but Tuck had come through his first big test with flying colours.

By the time he faced his first day of combat, Tuck had amassed more than 700 flying hours in the Spitfire and was thirsting for action. He had also survived a horrific mid-air collision while flying a Gladiator biplane in 1938. After this accident he had lain in hospital for six weeks, and was left with a nasty scar on his face, but he lived to fight again.

❖ ❖ ❖

At the end of Tuck's first day of combat in May 1940, his entire squadron had totalled twenty enemy kills for the loss of five of their own craft. The lost pilots included their squadron leader, Roger Bushell. Tuck was put in charge of the squadron the very next day as they flew similar missions, called sorties, over Dunkirk. He immediately made an important change – the Spitfires were to fly further apart, in looser formations, in order to make them a less obvious target.

During the day, 92 Squadron attacked a group of German bombers. Tuck singled out a Dornier Do-17 bomber and riddled its side and wing with bullets from his plane's eight machine guns. As he closed in for the kill, the Dornier's turret gunners returned fire, hitting the British pilot in the leg. The pain was sharp but Tuck tried to ignore it. He closed in and despatched the German bomber with more bursts from his aircraft's machine guns.

Despite his aircraft running low on fuel and ammunition, and the pain from his leg, Tuck took on another bomber of the same type and shot this down as well before limping back to his home airfield. A doctor was rushed in to look after his wound but Tuck couldn't be stopped. He was up again the very next day, leading the squadron out on sorties.

Tuck received the Distinguished Flying Cross (DFC) from King George VI the following month for his 'initiative' and 'personal example' over Dunkirk. He quickly became a personal hero to other, less experienced flyers on account of his great skill in the air.

❖　❖　❖

Later in the summer of 1940, during a lull in the fighting, Tuck was sent to the Vickers aircraft company to have a new camera and gun fitting attached to his Spitfire. On the way back, he stopped off at RAF Northolt and was having some lunch when the air raid warning sirens sounded. The Luftwaffe had launched a major attack on RAF airfields in the south of England. Tuck was ordered to the safety of an air raid bunker, but instead hopped into his Spitfire and was airborne within minutes. He joined the most enormous dogfight as a mass of RAF Spitfires and Hurricanes and

German bombers and fighters whirled in the air.

Tuck spied two Junkers Ju88 bombers, chased them out to sea and shot one of them down. He followed up by attacking the second one head on, but the enemy plane's nose gunner caught Tuck's Spitfire in his sights and blew half his propeller away as well as hitting his oil tank.

Gritting his teeth, Tuck knew he was in trouble but continued to focus on the bomber looming in his sights. He kept his aircraft travelling dead straight, with his machine guns blazing. It was the ultimate, deadly serious, game of chicken – the two aircraft were almost upon each other with neither pilot backing off and giving way. At the very last moment, they just managed to avoid a mid-air collision, the Spitfire's wing scraping over the top of the German bomber's.

The fate of Ju88 is lost to history but Tuck's Spitfire was in desperate shape. Oil was spurting all over the body of the plane, and the engine was screaming and grinding itself into a mess. The cockpit instrument dials had long since entered the red (or danger) zones, and Tuck silently thanked Rolls Royce for building a Merlin engine that was tough enough to keep his Spitfire going, despite being shot to pieces.

❖　❖　❖

Using all the skill he had built up over hundreds of hours flying Spitfires, Tuck managed to guide the wounded aircraft back towards the English coast. Much of his navigation was guesswork; he could see precious little, as the windscreen was thick with oil.

Then, just as he spied land below him and was thinking about which airfield he might be able to reach, the engine died and raw heat leapt up at him from below the cockpit. He had only seconds. As he wrenched the glass canopy back, smoke started to billow out of the cockpit and flames leapt at Tuck's legs. A spurt of hot oil hit him in the face, making him choke and splutter.

With a massive, last effort, Tuck hauled himself over the side of the Spitfire and out into freefall. He fumbled for and jerked the ripcord of his parachute which billowed open not long before he hit the ground. He was well below the minimum height for parachute safety and, on landing, badly wrenched his leg. His Spitfire had crashed in flames several hundred metres away at almost the same time.

It turned out that Tuck had landed in the Kent grounds of Lord Cornwallis. And after he'd had a bath and a doctor had been called, he had tea with his Lordship and his family. Tuck knew he had been extremely fortunate. If his plane had been any lower, or he had been any slower to pull his parachute cord, he would probably not have survived to tell the tale.

True stories such as these made Tuck a living legend but he remained modest about his actual flying abilities and preferred to use 'Tuck's Luck' to explain away his successes. Others knew the truth. He may have had his share of luck but he was a daring, brave and exceptional fighter pilot. He also became an inspirational leader.

❖   ❖   ❖

On 11 September, less than a month after his near-death combat experience, Tuck took command of a squadron in complete disarray; 257 Squadron had made relatively few kills but had lost many of its best pilots throughout July and August. The squadron were equipped with Hurricane fighters whose main job was to attack the German bombers threatening to bomb Britain into submission.

Tuck's first flights in a Hurricane filled him with dread. The Hurricane was slower and harder to manoeuvre than his beloved Spitfire. Although he did not say so at the time, Tuck felt that he was piloting a 'flying brick'. However, he flew as many times as he could in the slower but robust plane and gradually discovered its advantages. It was more stable than the Spitfire when its guns were firing and could take more punishment, yet still keep on flying. With this first-hand knowledge of his new plane and with his understanding of war in the air, Tuck drilled and instructed his squadron rigorously in the few days they had before they were to resume battle.

❖ ❖ ❖

Tuck led 257 Squadron into combat at the very height of the Battle of Britain. With so little time to turn things around, it could have been a disaster, yet the squadron became a celebrated unit responsible for many successful sorties, and Tuck was recognised as a brave and skilful soldier. In January of 1941, Tuck was awarded the Distinguished Service Order (DSO) for his leadership, but preferred to think of it as a reward for the pilots and engineers who had made 257 Squadron such a formidable fighting unit. The truth was that Tuck's value as a skilled pilot in the air was beginning to be outweighed by his importance as a teacher of newer, less experienced pilots.

Throughout 1941, he helped train all nationalities of Allied pilots in the latest combat moves and tactics, including squadrons of newly arrived American pilots. There was no way, however, that the authorities could persuade him to take a ground job. He loved being in the air and, having survived so many life-threatening situations, he knew of the risks more than most. Throughout much of 1941, he flew in combat missions, claiming more than a dozen further kills.

❖   ❖   ❖

Tuck was now promoted to Wing Commander and put in charge of a number of fighter squadrons based at Biggin Hill. In January 1942, he was just over the coast of mainland Europe, using cannon fitted to his Spitfire to attack an alcohol manufacturing plant, when he was caught in the middle of a storm of flak sent by an anti-aircraft battery on the ground. As the flak peppered the fuselage, Tuck wrestled to keep control of his aircraft. He pulled back the canopy and looked for a place to crash-land. But, before landing, he decided to make one more low-level sweep over the gun battery which had hit his plane and let them have a final burst of fire.

A successful crash-landing made, Tuck was captured in an instant but was treated exceptionally well. The Germans were impressed by his incredible marksmanship. He had, without realizing it, fired a cannon shell which had gone straight into the mouth of one of the guns, splitting and peeling the barrel back along its length.

Before he was sent to a prison camp in Germany, Tuck unexpectedly enjoyed an evening meal with the man who would later become head of the entire German fighter corps, General Adolf Galland. He and Galland discovered that they had fought each other in the air a year earlier, and had only just failed to shoot each other down. Their friendship was rekindled after the war and lasted for many decades.

❖ ❖ ❖

Tuck was now a prisoner of war but had absolutely no intention of remaining one for long. He was always polite and friendly but he was completely intent on escape and soon found himself at one of the camps for 'bad boys', the well-known Stalag Luft III. There he was reunited with his original squadron leader over Dunkirk, Roger Bushell. He was also down on the list as one of the men who would take part in what became known as the 'Great Escape', where seventy-six men left the camp using a tunnel they had carefully dug. But he was moved from the camp just days before the Great Escape took place. Nevertheless, at the beginning of 1945, Tuck successfully escaped from a prisoner of war camp in Poland and before the war's end he was back in Britain.

Despite being out of a fighter plane for three

years of the war, Tuck's tally of twenty-nine kills (a thirtieth was added in 1982 when the wreck of a Messerschmitt Me109 was found) still placed him eighth on the list of RAF aces. Many consider him one of the finest fighter pilots of World War II – a man who was gifted with good fortune, but who also used his skill and bravery to play an important part in the war in the air.

◆ ◆ ◆

CHAPTER 7

The Most Dangerous Man in Europe

Italy was Germany's main ally in Europe during World War II, but by 1943 its forces were crumbling. The Allies invaded the Italian island of Sicily on 10 July 1943. Several weeks later, Benito Mussolini was overturned as leader of Italy, placed under arrest, and secretly moved to a remote area. Security was so tight that not even Germany's network of spies in Italy knew his whereabouts.

Hitler and his generals put their plans into effect. Northern Italy and Rome had been captured by the Allies and secured, but Hitler wanted Mussolini found and rescued. He entrusted this mission to a fearless major who headed a newly formed division of German commandos – soldiers who had been specially trained to carry out amphibious (land and sea) raids. The British and American forces would come to know him as 'The most dangerous man in Europe'. His name was Otto Skorzeny.

◆　◆　◆

It was a mission that few of the German High Command thought could succeed. Two of the twelve gliders hadn't even managed to take off. The remainder would be attempting the gliding equivalent of landing on a handkerchief, aiming to set down on a desperately small, rocky plateau high in the Italian Abruzzi mountains. The risks were enormous, the chances of failure great, but the prize was a big one – the safety of Hitler's closest ally, Il Duce, otherwise known as Benito Mussolini.

Out in front, in the lead glider, Major Otto Skorzeny urged his men on. Unable to see through the heavy, blurred cellophane windows, he had already slashed a hole in the canvas fabric of the glider's body to view what lay ahead. As they neared their target, Skorzeny saw that the triangular mountain plateau was smaller than expected and dangerously angled. His superiors had told him to turn back if the landing area wasn't of good quality. This triangle of sloping granite wasn't, but he decided to press on.

It was now or never, thought Skorzeny and roared through the noise of air turbulence to make himself heard. 'Crash landing! As near to the hotel as you can get!' The glider pilot struggled with the controls and the passengers braced themselves.

Seconds later, the glider smashed into the landing site. Much of its body and wings was wrecked by the rocks which studded the plateau's surface. But these rocks also helped slow the aircraft down. It skidded to a halt and within moments the first man rolled out of the side hatch. Skorzeny followed.

❖　❖　❖

Letting himself fall sideways out of the glider, the major checked his weapons and surveyed the scene. The glider had landed no more than fifteen paces from the hotel. The Italian guards could not believe what they were seeing. They stood frozen in amazement as Skorzeny took action. He had previously ordered that no member of his crack force should fire a shot before he did. He hoped for as little bloodshed as possible. Barging his way into the hotel, he found an Italian soldier starting to transmit a warning message. Skorzeny kicked the man's chair from under him. A sharp jab from his rifle butt, and the radio was smashed.

As he vaulted up to a terrace landing, Skorzeny

spotted a shaven-headed figure at an upper window. It was Mussolini. 'Get back! Get back from the window!' Skorzeny shouted, and headed through the hotel and up the stairs. He burst into the room holding the Italian leader, followed by several of his men. The two Italian soldiers guarding Mussolini were surprised and the commandos overcame them with ease. Skorzeny turned to an equally surprised Mussolini and greeted him. 'Duce, the Führer has sent me! You are free!' Mussolini embraced his rescuer.

❖   ❖   ❖

Skorzeny was a tough, uncompromising soldier who spoke his mind, and often ruffled the feathers of senior officers. Born in the Austrian city of Vienna, he had attended his home city's university where he had studied engineering. A massive scar down the left side of his face was the result of a duel with swords while at university. This scar, combined with Skorzeny's bulk – he was almost 2 metres tall and strongly built – made him stand out in more ways than one. Yet Skorzeny was to become famous for his stealth and brilliant daring in commando raids rather than for his size and brute strength.

When the war started, Skorzeny joined an elite part of the German military, the Schutzstaffel (SS), and rose rapidly through the ranks. Having served in the invasions of Holland, France and the Balkan states, he was wounded during the 1941-42 invasion of Russia. Back in Germany, he was given a leading role in a new force which was to be modelled along British commando lines.

❖ ❖ ❖

Skorzeny had never even been in the same room as the German leader so he was astonished when he was one day called to meet Hitler in person. The Führer outlined the problem concerning Mussolini and how vital it was that he was rescued. Although nominally under the command of a senior general, Skorzeny himself was specifically entrusted with the task of locating and rescuing the Italian dictator.

Having attempted to discover Mussolini's whereabouts for a number of weeks, Skorzeny and others eventually discovered that he was being held in a hotel near the top of Gran Sasso mountain. The Hotel Campo Imperatore was incredibly isolated, perched on the side of the hostile mountain. There was no road to it and the only land link was a cable car that ran from the hotel to a small road a long way below.

Skorzeny, his second-in-command Karl Radl, and many others pored over maps and aerial photographs of Gran Sasso for some time. A decision had to be made and they had to act quickly, otherwise Mussolini might be moved, hurt, or even executed. Skorzeny believed that the only way of reaching Mussolini's hotel prison was by using gliders. The German High Command thought it was madness, but Skorzeny repeatedly challenged them to come up with a better plan. They couldn't and so, at around 1 p.m. on 12 September 1943, the gliders took off on their 100 kilometre journey to the mountain of Gran Sasso.

❖   ❖   ❖

Within minutes of encountering Mussolini, Skorzeny's soldiers had secured the area. The garrison of 250 soldiers was taken by surprise and speedily surrendered to Skorzeny's force of less than a hundred. Not a shot was fired and, apart from the ten men who died in one glider which crashed, there was no bloodshed. It was a remarkable operation, but it was far from complete. Mussolini still had to be transported safely away from his mountain prison.

Skorzeny quickly ran through the possible escape routes in his mind. The cable car – the only land route off the mountain and to a road – had been secured by Skorzeny's forces so Mussolini could be ferried by car to Rome or driven to a nearby airfield at Aquila. However, enemy forces would probably be swarming through both these areas. Skorzeny chose the third option, knowing all about its high risks. He was going to have Mussolini flown directly off the mountain. He signalled for the flimsy-looking Fiesler Storch reconnaisance aircraft circling overhead to come into land.

The pilot in the aircraft, Hauptmann Gerlach, was not pleased to hear of Skorzeny's decision. As he circled lower, Skorzeny's men cleared as many of the boulders and larger rocks as possible from the sloping mountain plateau to create a better landing area. The Storch had to make an emergency landing and damaged part of its under-carriage, but it reached its target.

On paper, the Fiesler Storch looked anything but impressive. It had a top speed of only 109 miles per hour, and could carry only the lightest of loads. But in the hands of a skilled and experienced pilot, it was very manoeuvrable and could land in the tightest of areas, as Gerlach had just proved.

Even so, the pilot would need to perform wonders to ferry three heavy men off the short, angled top of a mountain. The Storch was designed for no more than two people. In such a lightweight craft, an extra person would cause serious overloading. Gerlach thought it was suicide and began to argue with Skorzeny, but Skorzeny convinced him that there was no other option.

❖ ❖ ❖

Skorzeny personally accompanied Mussolini into the plane and strapped him in. The German commando crammed his large frame into the plane behind Mussolini and gripped the plane's body tightly. A number of Skorzeny's special force played tug-of-war with the Fiesler Storch. They held the tail and wings of the plane while Gerlach revved the engine to peak power. On a signal, they released their grip and the plane lurched forward along the plateau before running off the sheer edge of the mountain.

Over the cliff, the aircraft plunged. To those present, the plane seemed to disappear completely, as if to its doom. There was a second gasp from those watching. Skorzeny's friend and second-in-command, Karl Radl, lay slumped on the ground. He had fainted at the sight.

Down the plane plummeted. Mussolini said nothing, tightly strapped into his seat, while Skorzeny had to use all his strength to hold on to the frame of the diving aircraft. 'I was thinking that this really was the end,' recounted Skorzeny later on. The air screamed around the craft as it dropped and the plane shuddered with the force buffeting its light frame. In a flash, the plane levelled out just 30 metres above what would have been certain death. Plane and pilot had come through but still had work to do. The front left part of the plane's undercarriage was mangled and, on arriving at Rome, Gerlach had to perform yet another emergency landing on two wheels.

❖ ❖ ❖

Travelling in a Heinkel 111 bomber from Rome to Vienna was a far more comfortable ride for Mussolini and Skorzeny. Arriving in Skorzeny's home city, the pair were shown to the grandest hotel in the city. The aging Italian leader was exhausted and went straight to bed. Soon he would form a new government in northern Italy, largely under German control. But there was to be no rest for Skorzeny.

A colonel in charge of Vienna's forces appeared and took his Knight's Cross medal from his own neck and placed it around Skorzeny's. 'I am here on the orders of the Führer', he announced. It was the first time anyone had ever received such a high decoration on the actual day he had won it. Moments later, the phone in Skorzeny's room rang. It was the German leader speaking from his Wolf's Lair.

'You have performed a military feat which will become part of history,' exclaimed a delighted Hitler who promoted him on the spot to Sturm-bannführer (the German equivalent of Major).

❖　❖　❖

This was by no means the last of Skorzeny's exploits; he was involved in three further famous operations during the war. In July 1944, he took part in the counter-attack in Berlin which prevented the overthrow of Hitler by Stauffenberg and others (see Chapter 3). Then, three months later, he was again personally summoned by Hitler. The leader of Hungary, one of German's few European allies, was secretly negotiating peace with Russia. This would spell disaster for the Nazis led by Hitler, but, again, the dashing commando didn't let his leader down.

He flew to Hungary's capital, Budapest, and kidnapped the Hungarian leader's son by rolling him up in a carpet and hauling him off to the airport. When this didn't work, he went for the leader, Admiral Horthy himself, forcing the palace troops to surrender, before flying Horthy off to Berlin. A puppet government was installed, under German control, and Hungary stayed in the war on Hitler's side until the end.

Finally, in the winter of 1944, Skorzeny headed a force which had the aim of causing mass chaos and confusion behind the enemy front line. Called Operation Greif, the plan involved sending in hundreds of English-speaking German troops to spread misinformation, giving false orders and directing allied troops to wrong positions in order to disrupt the allies' progress. It was an outrageous move, attempted with precision and boldness typical of Skorzeny, but it was only a limited success.

❖ ❖ ❖

Even when the war had ended, Skorzeny's adventures continued. Ten days after peace had been declared in Europe in 1945, Skorzeny gave himself up to the Americans who had launched a massive search for 'The Most Dangerous Man in Europe'. Although he was put on trial he was found not guilty of any war crimes. However, because the Allied forces were fearful of what havoc this man could wreak, they held him prisoner long after his trial.

By 27 July 1948, Skorzeny had had enough and escaped by stowing away in a car boot. He disguised himself by bleaching his hair and eventually made it across the Atlantic Ocean to South America. For a time, he was a security adviser for Juan Peron, the leader of Argentina, and even acted as personal bodyguard to Peron's wife Eva, foiling at least one attempt on her life.

❖ ❖ ❖

Having survived the war, Skorzeny fled to Spain where he traded on his reputation as a war hero and outstanding combat leader. He helped form and run Odessa, an organization dedicated to helping many of his former Nazi comrades escape to South America. But he is most remembered for his wartime activities and particularly for that famous swoop on Gran Sasso – one of the most intrepid and successful raids by soldiers on any side during World War II.

In Mussolini's words, shortly after the raid, 'Tales of escape and rescue – dramatic, romantic, sometimes fantastic – are to be found in the history of every epoch and of every people; but my escape from the Gran Sasso prison appears as the boldest, the most romantic of all.'

◆ ◆ ◆

CHAPTER 8

The Cockleshell Heroes

'Not By Strength, By Guile.' This was the motto of the Special Boat Service (SBS). Founded in 1941, the SBS was the British Navy's equivalent of the army's Secret Air Service (or SAS), and took part in a number of audacious, top-secret raids and combat actions. Some of these were in tiny submersibles called X-craft or using frogmen equipped with primitive scuba diving equipment.

Another group, one of the first units of the SBS, was a special force of Royal Marines equipped with specially designed canoes. Their most famous raid on German ships in Bordeaux was eventually portrayed in a film which took its title from their real-life nickname, 'The Cockleshell Heroes'.

❖ ❖ ❖

Under cover of darkness, the sleek British submarine HMS *Tuna* gently broke the surface of the waters of the Bay of Biscay. Its task had to be completed quickly and quietly. The submarine was deep within the waters of German-held France and any delay would be fatal. There was a constant risk of detection from land, as well as from passing ships and fishing boats. The crew started to unload its precious cargo – ten men and five heavily laden canoes. There should have been six canoes and twelve men but one of the small craft had been damaged during the journey from Britain.

The five two-man canoes cautiously paddled their way across the Bay of Biscay hoping to remain unseen. They planned to head up the estuary – where the River Gironde flows out into the sea – and into the river itself. More than 80 kilometres further upstream was the port of Bordeaux, the target for the ten brave men of Operation Frankton.

❖ ❖ ❖

The Germans had a small but important fleet of vessels moored in a harbour at Bordeaux. These merchant ships were designed to overcome Allied attempts to block their journeys south, round the coast of Africa, to Japan. Ferrying weapons, ammunition and vital materials – such as tin, tungsten and raw rubber – to the German war effort, these blockade runners were lightly armed but too fast for the British submarines to catch and attack them. Nor would the Allied forces risk a high-altitude bombing raid by large bombers such as the Avro Lancaster or Short Stirling aircraft. High-level bombing was notoriously inaccurate and would more likely than not kill a lot of innocent French civilians.

Combined Operations in Britain were keen to stop the blockade runners, and considered sending an elite force of commandos into the area. But the port of Bordeaux was a long way inland, and commandos could only be ferried to and from the coast. But what if the explosives and soldiers could paddle their way up the river to the port? As crazy as it sounded, that was precisely what they planned, with the assistance of a special unit of the Royal Marines.

❖   ❖   ❖

The Royal Marines Boom Patrol Detachment (RMBPD) was an awfully long name but it was designed with secrecy in mind. The RMBPD was a small, thirty-strong force of Royal Marines led by Major H.G. 'Blondie' Hasler. They were trained as a raiding party using canoes to reach their target. When the idea had first been proposed, many senior soldiers had thought the idea ludicrous. But under Hasler, a keen sailor, who had built his first craft at the age of nine, the RMBPD trained hard and formed a tough, resourceful fighting unit.

'Blondie' Hasler, so-called because of his mass of blond hair, had helped design canoes specially for such missions. They became known as Cockle Mark IIs and gave rise to the unit's popular nickname, the 'Cockleshell Heroes'. The canoes sat low in the water so that they were hard to spot. Each of the canoes to be used in Operation Frankton was given its own name: Cuttlefish, Cachalot, Coalfish, Crayfish, Catfish and Conger. Cachalot was the vessel which was damaged on the journey from Britain.

❖ ❖ ❖

Disaster struck when the canoeists entered the churning waters of the estuary mouth. The waves roared, tossing the small vessels this way and that, and it looked as if they would all capsize in the savage surf. Conger was quickly sunk and lost. Coalfish followed. The remaining canoeists gritted their teeth and battled the raging tidal waters. Their mission was vital – they had to make it through this torrent and into the river proper.

Exhausted and coughing up seawater, only four men in two canoes stayed on course and reached safety, inside the river mouth. These were Catfish holding the raid's leader, Major Hasler, and Marine William Sparks, and Crayfish containing Corporal Laver and Marine Mills. The two canoes waited as long as they dared for any sign of Cuttlefish. Nothing emerged. With heavy hearts, the four canoeists slowly paddled away up the River Gironde.

The crew of Coalfish had drowned. The crew of Conger managed to swim to land, where they were captured by German forces. The same fate befell the crew of Cuttlefish which made it into the river mouth separately from the others.

It was the night of 7 December 1942 and already the mission looked doomed to failure. Only four men (rather than twelve) were left to make the raid on Bordeaux, and Bordeaux was still over 80 kilometres of hard, dangerous paddling away. They remembered how calm the crew on the HMS *Tuna* had been when they were attacked by a German U-boat on their journey to the Bay of Biscay. A strange sound in the sea near the submarine had caused one of the Cockleshell Heroes to ask, 'What was that?' The matter-of-fact reply had shocked the

Royal Marines, 'Oh, it was a German torpedo going past.' They needed the same level-headedness now. The four had to press on. They were on their own in enemy waters and there could be no turning back.

Each canoe carried almost 140 kilograms of kit, in addition to the two men, and paddling upstream was hard work. The pairs of canoeists had to force themselves almost to their limits to make enough progress during the night. As soon as it grew light, the travelling upstream had to stop. The men had to find a safe place to hide among the reeds or tucked under a high river bank.

For three days and three nights, this continued. The men were living on very basic food rations; they were wet through and exhausted. It was so cold that ice formed on the decks of their canoes. Several times, they were almost spotted by enemy forces. Once they were found, but fortunately it was by French villagers, sympathetic to the Allies.

❖ ❖ ❖

On 11 December, the crews of the Catfish and the Crayfish had reached their target. Hiding in a mass of tall reeds, the crews were able to brew up some tea and take stock of their position. In the distance across the river, the shapes of several large German merchant ships could be made out. That night, those ships would be their target. Spirits were high for the first time since the mission had begun. They were just a few hours away from their goal. The four men alternately slept and kept watch, hidden by the reeds, waiting for the sun to set and the skies to darken.

As night fell, the remaining members of Operation Frankton checked their cargo of explosives. Each canoe had eight limpet mines designed to attach to the steel hull of a ship and stay there until the fuse timer detonated them. The marines set the limpet fuses to approximately eight hours. When the time was up, the explosives would rip large holes in the merchant ships. By then, they hoped to be far away from the port.

❖ ❖ ❖

Just after 9 p.m., the two canoe crews shook each other's hands and wished each other luck. Laver and Mills in Crayfish headed off first. They were to attack the ships on one side of the river. Hasler and Sparks, in Catfish, would set mines on to ships in the docks on the other side.

The four canoeists paddled off and cursed the conditions. Instead of the usual cloudy, drizzly, December night with poor visibility, the night sky was clear and the moon lit the whole area. Hasler and Sparks paddled Catfish stealthily around the port, surveying their targets. There were seven cargo ships and tankers. The docks were well-lit but the ships cast deep shadows which the Catfish attempted to stay in as it crept its way around.

Sparks and Hasler picked their first target, a large cargo ship. They paddled close to its body so that anyone on deck would have to look right over to spot them. Sparks attached the canoe to the body of the cargo ship with a device called a magnetic anchor. Then Hasler attached the limpet mines, three in all, to different parts of the hull.

❖   ❖   ❖

The second target was a small German destroyer known as a 'sperrbrecher'. The pair were at work when, high above them, on the deck, a German sentry looked over the side. Shortly after, the beam of the sentry's torch swept the waters near them. Hasler and Sparks bent over their canoe and froze in position. They hoped their black clothing and canoe would melt into the shadows and dark waters of the dock. The torchlight rested over them. Surely the sentry had seen them.

The seconds passed agonizingly slowly. The canoe was now drifting alongside the destroyer's body and the torch seemed to follow them. Any movement would surely give the game away. The pair just had to sit tight and hope. With their heads down and their backs exposed, both Sparks and Hasler were scared. Would the crack of a rifle firing be the last sound they heard?

Sweet relief! The sentry had disappeared and no alarm had been sounded. Hasler placed another mine on the destroyer's hull and, with their hearts pounding furiously, they moved on to their next target.

Two ships were moored side by side and the marines had decided to attach the last of their mines to both ships. Suddenly a shift in the tides pressed on the outer ship, and the two giant steel vessels started to draw together. The flimsy canoe was caught in the middle. In seconds, it and the two men would be crushed by the enormous weight. Sparks and Hasler worked frantically – trying to hold the ships apart and squeeze themselves out of the way. Sparks was convinced they were going to die. But their luck held out. Another change in the swirling tides and the ships eased apart a little. Sparks and Hasler paddled as quickly and quietly as they could, out of harm's way.

❖   ❖   ❖

All eight of Hasler and Sparks' limpet mines were attached. The pair propelled Catfish quietly away from the ships. With the heavy limpet mines removed from their boat, the canoe was much lighter and paddling was easier. The two men stopped for a brief rest and were in joyous mood, until they heard movement in the water. They tensed themselves and gripped their weapons. But it was Laver and Mills in Crayfish. They, too, had attached their limpet mines successfully.

The four men congratulated each other before saying goodbye. By sunrise, the crews of the Catfish and Crayfish had paddled some distance away from Bordeaux. They had sunk their canoes and were making haste on land, looking to contact the French resistance as a means of refuge and eventual escape.

At 7 a.m., the first of the limpet mines exploded. The majority of the others went off between an hour and a half and two hours later. One of the mines didn't explode until one o'clock in the afternoon. The members of Operation Frankton were not close enough to witness the damage done but their attack proved successful. One of the ships sank immediately, while at least three others were very seriously damaged.

❖ ❖ ❖

Laver and Mills had travelled almost 30 kilometres on land before they were caught and handed over to the German Gestapo. They, like the four other captured canoeists, were executed by firing squad. Sparks and Hasler were luckier. They made contact with members of the French resistance and spent three months in hiding, before travelling in secret through southern France and into Spain. They finally arrived on the British island of Gibraltar in the Mediterranean in April 1943.

Hasler and Sparks were honoured back in Britain. Long before their return, the Allied forces had learned of the raid's relative success and the damage done to the cargo shipping. The price had been high. Of the ten men who had set out on the actual raid, two had drowned and six had been captured and – despite being uniformed soldiers – had been executed by the Germans. Only Sparks and Hasler survived to tell the tale, a story of great courage and endurance.

◆ ◆ ◆

CHAPTER 9

The One That Got Away

There are many well-known tales of Allied prisoners of war held in prisoner of war (POW) camps in occupied Europe by the Germans and Italians. A number managed to escape and journey across German-held territory to reach neutral countries like Switzerland, or even Britain. In many cases, the Allied escapers received help from local people in the occupied countries.

What is less well-known is that many German sailors and airmen were also captured and held prisoner in camps in Britain. Their chances of a successful escape back to Germany were almost zero, because they had to evade detection on an island nation with few or no sympathetic locals. In the early years of World War II, most German POWs therefore sat and waited patiently for Hitler's plan to invade Britain – Operation Sealion.

But one German flyer, Franz von Werra, was just too impatient. His cunning and resourcefulness made him the only German, captured in Britain, ever to escape and eventually make it back to Germany.

◆　◆　◆

A flight of Spitfires from RAF 234 squadron were patrolling the brightly lit skies above Kent when they spotted some anti-aircraft guns blazing away over the coastal town of Gravesend. Flying over to take a look, they spotted two German single-seat fighter planes, piloted by Erich von Selle and his second-in-command, Franz von Werra, and decided to surprise the Germans from above. Von Selle managed to dive out of the line of fire. But Von Werra was not so fortunate. The unmistakable rat-a-tat of machine-gun fire sounded as his Messerschmitt Me109 fighter plane was raked with bullet holes. His attacker was one of the British squadron commanders, Flight Lieutenant Paterson 'Pat' Hughes, an Australian ace.

Von Werra gripped the controls harder as he fought to evade the attacking Spitfire. He felt the engine of his plane lurch and splutter. His Me109 was badly hit and started to dive towards the ground. Pat Hughes wheeled round and chased the diving Messerschmitt. He was after the kill but von Werra managed to swerve and duck most of the further streams of bullets that came from the Spitfire's wing-mounted machine guns.

No more than 50 metres from the ground, von Werra just managed to level out his stricken plane. The Spitfire had pulled away but the German now faced another danger. He was far too low to the ground to consider baling out and using his parachute. There was only one thing for it – he would have to try a crash landing.

Von Werra cut the power to what remained of his engine and tried to level out the stricken plane as best as he could. The Me109 skimmed across the treetops as the German pilot saw a field where he could try to crash-land. Machine-gun fire from British anti-aircraft guns whistled past the plane. The fighter pilot braced himself for impact as his craft lurched into the ground and slid and bumped along, battering him to and fro in his cockpit.

When the aircraft eventually skidded to a halt, von Werra was only bruised. He thanked God for his good fortune while at the same time cursing his bad luck for being shot down. Immediately, he was intent on escape. He pulled back the canopy and leapt out of his mangled machine.

Soldiers armed with rifles were charging across the field towards him. He could try to outrun the men but he could not outstrip the speed of their rifle bullets. He quickly pulled out important papers from his flight suit pockets and set light to them. The papers were still blazing when the soldiers reached him and pointed their rifle barrels in his face. He was captured.

❖   ❖   ❖

Von Werra had crash-landed on the side of Winchet Hill, south of the Kent town of Maidstone on 5 September 1940. He was quickly put in the back of an army truck, under armed guard, and taken to Kent Police headquarters where he was jailed. But von Werra's spirits weren't dampened. He declared himself a leading ace and was quite happy to sign the autograph book of the son of a police sergeant excited to meet a real-life German flyer.

Von Werra played the part of a hero well. He was already well-known in Germany. He was dashing, if a little boastful, and loved to outdo other pilots and draw attention to himself. He portrayed himself as a member of the German aristocracy and titled himself a Baron, even though he was nothing of the sort and was actually born in Switzerland. He even kept a pet lion cub at his aerodrome base in Germany. He was a good pilot, though, and his honour had been offended by being forced down by an enemy aircraft. He vowed to escape but, during his interrogation in Kent and then back in London, he was so heavily guarded that no opportunity came his way.

This did not stop von Werra from using the time usefully. In between resisting the offers and tricks used to get him to give away important military information, the charming German pilot used all his wits to learn lots of details about the country he was being held in. Von Werra had been relieved that the British didn't use physical torture but he had to be alert to their other techniques for getting enemy secrets, from microphones being hidden in his cell to being jailed with a friendly Luftwaffe officer who turned out to be a British actor.

❖   ❖   ❖

By the end of September, the interrogation was finished. Von Werra had given little away and was transported to the one permanent POW camp for German officers in Britain at the time. It was situated at Grizedale Hall, and to the locals who lived nearby, it was known as the 'U-boat Hotel' as most of the prisoners were from German submarines.

Grizedale Hall was close to the villages of Coniston and Hawkshead in the beautiful but isolated Lake District. However, on the long, slow train and road journey to the old stately home, it wasn't the beauty of the scenery which caught von Werra's interest. The large forested areas did intrigue him though – they would offer good cover when he made his escape attempt.

For von Werra, it was truly a matter of 'when' and not 'if'. He had an unshakable belief that he would make it back to Germany somehow, and, unlike other German POWs, he was not convinced that Hitler's plan to invade Britain would bring them a quick release. As soon as he joined the other German prisoners, he sought out the commanding officer and told him of his plans to get back to Germany. Within two weeks he had a plan and was ready.

On 7 October, von Werra was on an afternoon exercise march along with twenty-three other German officers. He bided his time until a good moment for escape arrived. A horse and cart carrying fruit and vegetables provided him with the perfect shield from the armed soldiers escorting the Germans. Von Werra dived over a low stone wall and quietly crept away.

For almost six days he managed to evade a massive search by soldiers, police and local civilians. The BBC warned the entire country about the German prisoner's escape. At one point, two members of the Home Guard (the citizens' army formed in 1940 to help defend Britain) caught him sheltering in a stone hut but he managed to wrestle himself free and flee again. When he was eventually caught in the countryside, he was sentenced to twenty-one days' solitary confinement before being moved to a brand-new, higher-security camp.

❖ ❖ ❖

Von Werra's new home was at Swanwick in the Midlands. He wasted no time in learning about the area and plotting a new escape attempt, joining forces with a number of other Germans in digging a tunnel out of the camp. The work was slow and arduous and there was a constant risk of being discovered or the tunnel collapsing and suffocating those inside. Yet, after a month's work, the tunnel was complete.

At a quarter past eight in the evening, five days before Christmas, von Werra and the four other escapees shook hands and made their way through their escape tunnel. They split up and made their separate exits. Von Werra hid in a nearby barn until three o'clock in the morning before setting out across the lonely, quiet fields.

Von Werra's own plan was an outrageous one. He was going to make his way across country to the nearest RAF airfield where he planned to steal a

British aircraft and fly back to Germany. When he had told his fellow conspirators, they had roared with laughter but von Werra wasn't joking. On the contrary, his quick mind had figured that posing as a Dutch officer flying out of Dyce airfield in Scotland would provide him with excellent cover, while flying an Allied plane would offer him the quickest, easiest route out of Britain. He had worked out all the details of his cover story and had even made his own identification plates, called dog tags, out of a sandwich of cardboard and lead blackened with shoe polish.

❖   ❖   ❖

It was still dark when he reached some railway lines and found a train in a siding with a driver on board. This was the first test of his disguise. Von Werra spoke good English with an accent which made it seem possible that he was a Dutchman. 'I am Captain van Lott, formerly of the Royal Dutch Air Force,' von Werra calmly announced. He explained all the details he had worked out. His Wellington aircraft had been hit and he had been forced to crash-land. He needed to get to the nearest RAF base immediately.

Taken to a train station, von Werra needed all his charm and skill as he repeated his story first to more railwaymen and then to some police who had been called. When a vehicle was called to take him to RAF Hucknall, everything seemed to be going according to plan. Von Werra was not about to relax, though. He knew the biggest hurdle lay ahead. He still had to convince the airbase personnel to believe his story, and then lay his hands on an enemy aircraft. The German pilot never seemed to doubt that he would be able to fly a strange plane with no training.

However, von Werra's natural confidence was tested to the limit when he eventually faced Squadron Leader Boniface at RAF Hucknall. The squadron leader was suspicious. Parts of this strange Dutchman's story didn't seem quite right to him. He told von Werra to wait while he called through to the airbase at Dyce to confirm his story. As the RAF officer went to make the call, von Werra crept away and out into the crisp dawn air. He tried not to run but walked briskly out to the track around the edge of the airfield and found a group of buildings. Parked there was exactly what he wanted – a Hurricane fighter plane and, next to it, an engine starting device on a trolley called an accumulator.

Von Werra didn't know it but he was in a special part of the airfield used by Rolls Royce, the makers of the Merlin engines that powered both the Hurricane and Spitfire fighter planes. He saw a mechanic nearby and his mind raced. He decided to change his story to that of a new pilot ordered to take a practice flight in a Hurricane and strode confidently over to the mechanic. The mechanic had other ideas, though. He assumed that this Dutchman was the pilot called to ferry one of the Hurricane fighter planes to another airbase at White Waltham. Von Werra again had to use his wits to adjust his story for a third time as he signed some paperwork and was shown to another Hurricane. There was no engine starter near this aircraft. Von Werra hopped into the cockpit and waited while the mechanic trudged slowly away to get one.

Von Werra was on the edge of his nerves now. The mechanic seemed to take an age to return. The controls and instruments inside the cockpit were quite unlike his Messerschmitt but von Werra tried to calm himself by studying them and getting used to them as much as he could.

Suddenly he felt someone climb on to the wing of the aircraft. He relaxed. At last, the mechanic was back. He turned his head, only to spy the barrel of an RAF service revolver inches away from his head. It was Squadron Leader Boniface. He had made the call, discovered that the Dutchman was an impostor, and had come seaching for him.

Wearily, the German escaper clambered out of the Hurricane's cockpit and was marched back to the base buildings at gunpoint. There was no point in pretending any longer. Under armed guard, von Werra confessed who he was. He cursed his bad luck bitterly. He had got within a whisker of one of the most outrageous escapes of World War II, fleeing Britain in one of its own prized aircraft – a feat that would have been a first as well as making him a national hero back in Germany.

Von Werra's re-capture was a source of great relief to the British authorities but they were still very embarrassed and no less than five separate inquiries and investigations rumbled on long after von Werra had served his second period of solitary confinement and had been packed on to a ship bound for Canada.

❖　❖　❖

Von Werra was one of over 33,000 German prisoners shipped out to Canada and away from the war in Europe. For almost all German prisoners, the thousands of kilometres put between them and their home country signalled the end of their escape attempts. But not for Franz von Werra. He made yet another bid for freedom, leaping from a train in Canada and sneaking across the border with the United States before giving himself up to US police in January 1941.

His arrival in the United States was a big news event and caused uproar back in Britain. Von Werra was at his most boastful, and exaggerated parts of his escape story. At this stage, the United States had yet to enter World War II and wondered what they should do with the charming German flyer. Should he be handed back to the Canadians or deported back to Germany?

With his fate hanging in the balance, von Werra didn't wait for a decision. He stole out of New York and managed to get to Mexico almost before the authorities started searching for him. A journey through Panama, Peru, Bolivia and Argentina followed, before he managed to get a flight from Argentina across the Atlantic. By the end of April 1941, von Werra was back in Germany and hailed as a genuine hero.

His return was a valuable propaganda victory but, more importantly, von Werra passed on everything he had learned during his time in enemy territory. His knowledge of interrogation techniques proved particularly useful to the Germans and, for a time, von Werra became an adviser to the commandants of prisoner of war camps. Yet he still thirsted for front-line action and returned to being a fighter pilot. He was soon commanding officer of a German fighter unit (1/JG 53) operating on the Russian front.

On 25 October 1941, his Messerschmitt Me109's engine failed and he plunged into the sea off the Dutch coast. There was to be no final escape for the dashing fighter pilot. Franz von Werra drowned, aged twenty-seven.

◆ ◆ ◆

Glossary

Allies Britain, the United States, the Soviet Union and twenty-three other countries that fought the Axis powers during World War II.

Altitude the height above the ground that an aircraft travels at.

Assassination murder of a military or political leader.

Axis Powers in 1936, Germany and Italy combined to form the Axis, which was joined by Japan and other opponents of the Allies during World War II.

border the boundary line between two countries.

camouflage ways of painting and disguising soldiers, bases and military equipment to make them hard for the enemy to spot.

commandos soldiers specially trained to carry out amphibious (land and sea) raids.

convoy a number of supply-carrying vehicles, usually ships or trucks, escorted and protected by military forces.

depth charge anti-submarine bomb dropped from ships and designed to explode underwater.

diversion a military move to attract enemy attention to one area while a more important military operation occurs in another.

flak fire from anti-aircraft guns.

Führer German for 'leader', the title used by Adolf Hitler.

genocide deliberate destruction of a racial, religious, political or ethnic group. Nazi Germany commited genocide, killing over 6 million Jews.

Gestapo much-feared German secret police who used brutal force and torture against those suspected of opposing the Nazi regime.

glider aircraft without an engine, used in wartime to land a small number of troops quietly, without alerting the enemy.

Kreigsmarine German submarine force.

Luftwaffe German air force.

morale the mood or confidence of soldiers or the public.

occupation the takeover and control of a country by a foreign military power.

offensive a major attack, involving many soldiers, on an enemy's line.

propaganda the use of speeches, newspapers and other media to influence people's attitudes and emotions.

prototype a trial model or test version of a machine such as an aircraft.

reconnaissance an inspection or exploration of an area, especially one made to gather military information.

refugee a person who is driven from their home and country.

reinforcements extra troops and equipment sent to join a military force.

retreat withdraw and go back into safer territory.

sentry a soldier acting as a guard, protecting an area or person.

SS abbreviation of Schutzstaffel, an élite part of the German military, which began as Hitler's personal bodyguard and expanded into a 250,000-strong organization with huge police and military powers.

torpedo a cigar-shaped missile fired from submarines, used mainly to sink shipping.

tracer bullet a type of bullet which emits a flame or trail to illuminate its path.

U-boat abbreviation of unterseeboot (underwater boat); name given to German submarines.

undercarriage the wheels and mechanism below an aircraft's body, used for landing and taking off.

volunteers people who offer to perform a task or join the armed forces without being ordered to by the authorities.

Further reading

Chapter 1:
Hitler's U-Boat War, Clay Blair
Weidenfeld & Nicolson, 2000

Chapter 2:
Women of Action: Code Name Pauline, Pearl Cornioley
Chicago Review, 2013
Women Heroes of World War II, Kathryn Atwood
Chicago Review Press, 2011

Chapter 3:
Operation Valkyrie, Pierre Galante
Cooper Square Press, 2002

Chapter 4:
The Official Dambusters Experience, John Sweetman
Carlton Books Ltd, 2013

Chapter 5:
PT109: John F. Kennedy in World War II, Robert Donovan
McGraw Hill, 2002

Chapter 6:
World War II Pilots: An Interactive History Adventure,
Michael Burgan, Capstone Press, 2013

Chapter 7:
Skorzeny: The Most Dangerous Man in Europe,
Charles Whiting, Pen & Sword Military, 2010

Chapter 8:
Cockleshell Heroes: The Final Witness, Quentin Rees
Amberley Publishing, 2010

Chapter 9:
The One That Got Away, Kendal Burt and James Leasor,
Pen & Sword Military, 2006

General:

*Beyond the Call of Duty: Bravery and Heroism in World
War II,* (in assocation with the National Archives), Peter
Hicks, Wayland, 2013

What They Don't Tell You About: World War II,
Bob Fowke, Wayland, 2013

Resources

The Royal Air Force Museum:
Grahame Park Way, Hendon, London, NW9 5LL.
Tel: 030 8205 2266
www.rafmuseum.org.uk

The Royal Air Force Museum:
Cosford, Shifnal, Shropshire, TF11 8UP
Tel: 01902 376200
www.rafmuseum.org.uk

Imperial War Museum:
Lambeth Road, London, SE1 6HZ
Tel: 020 7416 5374
www.iwm.org.uk

Imperial War Museum North:
The Quays, Trafford Wharf Road, Trafford Park,
Manchester, M17 1TZ
Tel: 0161 836 4000
www.iwm.org.uk

BBC History Online:
www.bbc.co.uk/history/worldwars/wwtwo

www.onwar.com:
A website with materials on World War II tanks
and battles as well as maps of different campaigns.

Index